CAMBRIDGE LIBRARY COLLECTION

Books of enduring scholarly value

History of Oceania

This series focuses on Australia, New Zealand and the Pacific region from the arrival of European seafarers and missionaries to the early twentieth century. Contemporary accounts document the gradual development of the European settlements from penal colonies and whaling stations to thriving communities of farmers, miners and traders with fully-fledged administrative and legal systems. Particularly noteworthy are the descriptions of the indigenous peoples of the various islands, their customs, and their differing interactions with the European settlers.

Narrative of Some Passages in the History of Van Diemen's Land

The famous explorer of the Arctic region, Sir John Franklin (1786–1847) was appointed Governor of the penal colony of Tasmania (then known as Van Diemen's Land) in 1837. At first enthusiastically welcomed by the free colonists of the island, Franklin quickly became embroiled in political and administrative difficulties, and his compassion for convicts and aboriginals alike was incompatible with his duties. In 1843, colonial officials loyal to his predecessor succeeded in getting Franklin recalled by sending damaging accounts of his conduct to London. This pamphlet was Franklin's defence of his own character against these misrepresentations, but he was not to see his reputation recovered. He completed the book on 15 May 1845, just days before he departed on another Arctic expedition to search for the North-West Passage. Franklin and his entire crew died on the journey, and only many years later was the tragic fate of the expedition discovered.

T0345399

Cambridge University Press has long been a pioneer in the reissuing of out-of-print titles from its own backlist, producing digital reprints of books that are still sought after by scholars and students but could not be reprinted economically using traditional technology. The Cambridge Library Collection extends this activity to a wider range of books which are still of importance to researchers and professionals, either for the source material they contain, or as landmarks in the history of their academic discipline.

Drawing from the world-renowned collections in the Cambridge University Library and other partner libraries, and guided by the advice of experts in each subject area, Cambridge University Press is using state-of-the-art scanning machines in its own Printing House to capture the content of each book selected for inclusion. The files are processed to give a consistently clear, crisp image, and the books finished to the high quality standard for which the Press is recognised around the world. The latest print-on-demand technology ensures that the books will remain available indefinitely, and that orders for single or multiple copies can quickly be supplied.

The Cambridge Library Collection brings back to life books of enduring scholarly value (including out-of-copyright works originally issued by other publishers) across a wide range of disciplines in the humanities and social sciences and in science and technology.

Narrative of Some Passages in the History of Van Diemen's Land

During the Last Three Years
of Sir John Franklin's
Administration of its Government

JOHN FRANKLIN

CAMBRIDGE
UNIVERSITY PRESS

CAMBRIDGE UNIVERSITY PRESS

Cambridge, New York, Melbourne, Madrid, Cape Town,
Singapore, São Paolo, Delhi, Mexico City

Published in the United States of America by Cambridge University Press, New York

www.cambridge.org
Information on this title: www.cambridge.org/9781108049757

© in this compilation Cambridge University Press 2012

This edition first published 1845
This digitally printed version 2012

ISBN 978-1-108-04975-7 Paperback

This book reproduces the text of the original edition. The content and language reflect
the beliefs, practices and terminology of their time, and have not been updated.

Cambridge University Press wishes to make clear that the book, unless originally published
by Cambridge, is not being republished by, in association or collaboration with, or
with the endorsement or approval of, the original publisher or its successors in title.

NARRATIVE

OF

SOME PASSAGES IN THE HISTORY

OF

VAN DIEMEN'S LAND,

DURING THE LAST THREE YEARS OF
SIR JOHN FRANKLIN'S ADMINISTRATION OF ITS GOVERNMENT.

NOT PUBLISHED.

PRINTED BY RICHARD AND JOHN E. TAYLOR,
RED LION COURT, FLEET STREET.

PREFACE.

THE following pages have been written chiefly for my friends in Van Diemen's Land, in order not to leave them in ignorance of the steps which I have taken to vindicate the honour of my late office, and my character as their Governor, from ex-parte representations on points on which, so long as I exercised the functions of government, I was precluded from offering any explanations.

Misrepresentations therefore long remained to a great degree uncontradicted by myself and unrefuted by my friends, not from want of good will on their part, but from want of a sufficient knowledge of all the facts.

The especial reference I have made to Van Diemen's Land will account for much minuteness and many circumstantial details which may seem somewhat tedious and obscure to those of my readers less informed and less interested in local matters than my Tasmanian friends. But there is not a single observation, however trivial, which is not intended to meet some special point on which studious misrepresentation has either been made or may be anticipated.

I have ventured on no statements which I cannot prove, though I have refrained in many instances from bringing the proof forward, either from consideration to individuals whose interests might be compromised, or from the regard which I consider due to the confidence of social intercourse.

A few words may be necessary to account for the delay in the appearance of the pamphlet. When all hope of any satisfactory adjustment of my differences with the Colonial Office was at an end, and the only alternative left me was a resort to the present step, circumstances of too private a nature to enter into here, unavoidably prevented its commencement.

The work most reluctantly begun has occupied more time than I had anticipated. It was very far from being finished when the preparations for the Arctic expedition called off my thoughts and time to other duties more congenial to my habits, and still more imperative ; and thus it has happened that, to my extreme vexation and regret, I find the day of my departure at hand without the satisfaction I had expected of seeing my pamphlet out of the press. This delay has however given me the advantage of receiving from Van Diemen's Land the documents contained in the Postscript. I have had this part of the work printed off, and have enclosed a copy to the Secretary of State for the Colonies.

In executing a task which has been exceedingly painful to me and altogether foreign to my tastes and habits, I trust it will be found that I have studiously avoided the introduction of matter inculpating others, except where it could not be avoided without destroying the integrity of my narrative, or where it was required in justice to myself.

I have disclaimed throughout, and do again disclaim, the existence of any vindictive feelings either towards the individual, my differences with whom have laid the foundation of my present act of self-defence, or towards any others, and I close my work under circumstances which will give to this assurance a depth and a seriousness to which words so easily uttered may not always be strictly entitled.

With respect to the Minister whose name I have been compelled to bring forward so frequently in the following pages, I trust it will be found that I have not been altogether unmindful of my late official subordination to him, nor of the respect which I consider due from a commissioned officer of Her Majesty's service to a member of the ministry under which he has the honour to serve.

JOHN FRANKLIN.

40 Lower Brook Street,
15th May, 1845.

SOME PASSAGES

IN

THE HISTORY OF

VAN DIEMEN'S LAND.

No. 150. DESPATCH.

Downing-street, 13th September, 1842.

SIR,

I HAVE received the series of Despatches, enumerated in the

No.	2. 27th Jan.	1842.	margin, reporting the various
No.	3. 8th Feb.	1842.	occurrences which led to the
No.	4. 9th Feb.	1842.	suspension from office of Mr.
No.	7. 18th Feb.	1842.	Montagu, the Colonial Secre-
No.	9. 18th Feb.	1842.	tary of Van Diemen's Land,
No.	14. 22nd Feb.	1842.	and to the arrival of that gen-
No.	18. 26th Feb.	1842.	tleman in this country.
No.	19. 1st March	1842.	This voluminous mass of
No.	33. 5th March	1842.	papers has occupied much of

my time, and has engaged my deliberate attention. In proceeding
to announce to you the decision at which I have arrived, I shall
not attempt to enter with any minuteness into the various details
and circumstances of the transactions to which they refer. Un-

B

fortunately the merits of the question are already so much darkened by the redundancy of the discussions in which it has been involved, that any addition to their length or number would rather increase than dissipate the obscurity. I shall therefore confine myself to a brief recapitulation of the charges preferred against Mr. Montagu, and to a statement of the conclusions which I have adopted respecting each of them.

1st. You have represented in substance (I purposely abstain from the quotation of the pages over which the complaint is spread), that Mr. Montagu had acquired an influence and authority in the administration of the affairs of your Government far exceeding that which properly belonged to his office; that this influence was maintained by means which, if not culpable, were at least objectionable, and was used in such a manner as to render his continued employment incompatible with the freedom and independence of action which the Lieutenant-Governor ought to maintain.

I am not disposed to controvert, but rather to adopt your opinion, that various circumstances had concurred to place in the hands of Mr. Montagu a degree of personal authority, which if not balanced by great energy and decision in his immediate superior, would probably tend to invert the relations which ought to subsist between them. But I find no reason to impute to Mr. Montagu the blame of having acquired this power by any unworthy means or dishonest arts; or of having employed it for any sinister purpose, or in an unbecoming spirit.

2nd. It is represented that when you overruled Mr. Montagu's advice in the case of Dr. Coverdale, Mr. Montagu manifested his discontent by words and by a course of conduct unbefitting his position and yours, disrespectfully intimating that the zeal which he had till then exhibited in the performance of his duty would be relaxed; and carrying that intimation into effect under such circumstances as to justify the belief that it was his design to embarrass you, by suddenly exposing you to what he esteemed insuperable difficulties.

I am not able entirely to acquit Mr. Montagu of having, in reference to Dr. Coverdale's case, employed some language which you not unnaturally regarded as a menace, or of having ceased to render you his efficient services in the same cordial and zealous spirit which, till then, he had been accustomed to evince towards you. It may be difficult to condemn a public servant who faithfully and ably performs whatever lies within the strict range of his duty, for not advancing further and yielding the aid which public spirit would prompt, or which a stronger personal regard for his superior would suggest. But the abrupt abandonment of a cordial co-operation for a service confined within the exact limits of positive duty may be the subject of a legitimate reproach, and from that reproach Mr. Montagu is not, I think, altogether to be exempted.

3rd. Mr. Montagu is charged with having made an improper use, in the course of these proceedings, of the name of a lady the most intimately allied to yourself.

I pass as rapidly as possible from such a topic, confining myself to the single remark, that the imputation does not appear to me to be well-founded.

4th. The next ground of accusation is Mr. Montagu's neglect to take proper notice of articles insulting to yourself and your family, which appeared in a newspaper established under his auspices and for which he had obtained your patronage, and his having by his conduct given countenance to the opinion that he had some personal connexion with these injurious paragraphs.

After fully weighing every part of this case, I entirely acquit Mr. Montagu of all connexion with the offensive articles in question, or with the authors of them, or of having done anything to promote such publications, or having omitted to do anything which, from his position in reference to yourself and your Government, might reasonably have been expected of him to prevent and discourage them.

5th. You complain of the language addressed by Mr. Montagu to your private secretary and to yourself, on the subject of these newspaper paragraphs, as having been wanting in the respect which it was his duty to observe towards you, and as having, in one instance, conveyed an insulting imputation on your credibility.

On this part of the case, also, I think that Mr. Montagu is entitled to be entirely acquitted of blame. He did indeed make use of an inadvertent expression in one of his letters to you, but the frankness and earnestness with which the error was acknowledged, and with which your forgiveness was solicited, seem to me to have been an ample atonement for an unfortunate selection of words; for such, and not any intentional insult, was the real character of the offence.

6th. It is imputed to Mr. Montagu, that he made an improper appeal against your suspension of him to the public at large, through the local newspapers, at the very moment when he was contemplating a return to this country to prefer his appeal to myself.

I think that he has fully exculpated himself from this accusation.

Finally, you represent that Mr. Montagu authorized the expenditure of large sums of public money in erecting the tower and spire of a church, not merely without your authority, but with a studious intention of keeping you in the dark on the subject.

Here, again, I think that Mr. Montagu is entitled to be completely absolved of the fault imputed to him. He had no notice of the charge before leaving Van Diemen's Land, but he has since repelled it to my entire satisfaction.

The result of my consideration of the whole subject is, as you will see, to relieve Mr. Montagu from every censure which impugns the integrity or the propriety of his conduct, while I am compelled to admit that the circumstances of the case are such as to render his restoration to his office in Van Diemen's Land highly inexpedient. It was therefore gratifying to me to have it in my power to offer him an equivalent, which, while it would mark my undiminished confidence in his disposition and ability to render effective public service, would direct his talents to a field of labour in which they could be exerted without the inconvenience which must attend his resumption of his duties as Colonial Secretary at Van Diemen's Land.

I offered for his acceptance the vacant office of Colonial Secretary at the Cape of Good Hope, and he has cheerfully accepted it. It cannot be too distinctly understood, that Mr. Montagu retires from the situation he has so long filled with his public and personal character unimpaired, and with his hold on the respect and confidence of Her Majesty's Government undiminished.

Mr. Bicheno has been appointed to succeed Mr. Montagu at Van Diemen's Land, and his arrival may be expected shortly after your receipt of this despatch.

I am not aware it could answer any useful purpose to enter more fully into the merits of this protracted controversy. But, reluctant as I am to employ a single expression which is likely to be unwelcome to you, I am compelled to add that your proceedings in this case of Mr. Montagu do not appear to me to have been well-judged, and that your suspension of him from office is not, in my opinion, sufficiently vindicated.

I have the honour to be, Sir,

Your most obedient humble servant,

STANLEY.

To Sir John Franklin, &c.

THE above document is my text for the observations contained in the following pages, and my apology for giving them circulation. The Despatch in question, addressed by the Secretary of State for the Colonies to myself, was made by his lordship to answer a double purpose. It not only served for the expression of his judgment to myself, but was officially transmitted to the late Colonial Secretary of Van Diemen's Land as the official answer to that gentleman's defence; and he received no other. Hence its circulation and publication in Van Diemen's Land whilst I was still administering the functions of government, and its subsequent re-appearance in a London newspaper at a period preceding by a short interval my return to England.

A few months after the arrival and circulation in Van Diemen's Land of this Despatch, a key to it and commentary was sent by Mr. Montagu to the colony in the form of a libellous manuscript, reflecting upon my character and honour and on that of Lady Franklin, and purporting to be minutes of conversations which Mr. Montagu had with Lord Stanley *before the Despatch was written*; or the substance of statements made verbally to his lordship by Mr. Montagu, in the interviews with which he was honoured by his lordship in Downing-street.

The manuscript was extensively circulated in this country and in Van Diemen's Land, and the fact of such conversations having taken place has not been repudiated by Lord Stanley, nor has Mr. Montagu's conduct been disapproved of.

Under these circumstances, the reserve which my position imposed upon me whilst I still administered the Government of the colony, and which afterwards both duty and policy forbade me to violate, so long as I had any hope of redress or counteraction from Lord Stanley, seems to me no longer possible. It is not without infinite pain and reluctance that I adopt the only alternative which remains to me.

My administration of the Government of Van Diemen's Land extended to a period of somewhat more than six years and a half, and the services of Mr. Montagu under it as Colonial Secretary occupied somewhat less than three years of that period. It is to the first two years, before he went on leave of absence to England, that the observations I am first about to make, apply.

On arriving in the colony, fully aware of the existence of strong party feeling which distracted it, and to which repeated allusions were made in the addresses with which I was presented; aware too that much was expected from me in counteraction of the policy of the late administration, and that it was my duty to be on my guard against the errors into which any hasty judgment on this head might easily lead a man of my inexperience in colonial government, I determined not to disturb the policy of my predecessor without necessity, yet to lose no time in learning and judging for myself.

The administration of Sir George Arthur had met with His Majesty's approbation. Though the Government of Van Diemen's Land had not been to him a bed of roses, yet every appeal against his acts and measures in Downing-street had signally failed. It was the wisdom of the Colonial Office in that day, so long as a governor was retained in office to support him; and that Sir George Arthur's policy had claims to recommend itself to my imitation could scarcely be doubted, not only from this test of its merit, but also from the unusual length of time he had been retained in the Government. This protracted administration, extending to double the usual period, had come in aid of other causes to give to my predecessor a degree of influence and power unknown to any other governor under the crown *.

I would not be understood to cast the slightest imputation on the exercise, by my distinguished predecessor, of his peculiar privileges, when I assert that the power which the head of the Government then possessed, to grant crown lands, and to assign unlimited supplies of convict labour, was sufficient to enable

---

* Except perhaps the similarly-situated Governor of New South Wales.

him to make or to mar the fortunes of any individual under his Government.

This unbounded patronage did not descend to me. I succeeded however to the inheritance of many a troublesome case, consequent upon the cessation of the free-grant system, and many an importunate appeal for the reconsideration of former judgments; and in these, the opinions of my predecessor and the advice of those of his officers who were best acquainted with the subject had necessarily to be consulted.

A new Governor on entering into office does not, like a new prime minister, form his own cabinet; he works with the instruments he finds around him, and who for a time have a great advantage over him from their superior local knowledge and experience.

It is not to be wondered at that I found the chief places of influence and emolument in Van Diemen's Land filled by the relatives and friends of the late Lieutenant-Governor. They formed a compact and strong body of connexions and adherents bound to their late chief by the ties of obligation and gratitude, and by that *esprit de corps* which ever exists where opposition is active and in any degree prevailing.

The office of Chief Police Magistrate, which in a penal colony and under the then existing system of convict management was one of great importance, was occupied by Mr. Forster; and the still more influential office of Colonial Secretary, through whom all correspondence between the Governor and the departments of Government, or between him and the colonists, is carried on, was filled by Mr. Montagu. These gentlemen had married two sisters, nieces of Sir George Arthur, and owed entirely to him their occupation of offices which are almost invariably in the present day filled from home. They were by virtue of their offices members of the Legislative and Executive Councils, and in both, but especially in the Executive Council, which consists of only six individuals, their influence was very generally felt.

These gentlemen had been particularly recommended to me, together with several other members of his government, by my predecessor. I found them possessed of much talent for business and of great local knowledge. Mr. Montagu, of whom I have chiefly now to speak, was thoroughly acquainted with the affairs and resources of the colony, with the interests and private affairs of individuals, and with the technical machinery of government.

He had, during a residence of twelve years in the colony, risen through the successive offices of Private Secretary and Clerk of the Councils to those of Treasurer and Colonial Secretary, the last two in consequence of the suspension by my predecessor of the officers holding those appointments*.

Mr. Montagu had also another source of influence. This was his money-agencies in connexion with the Derwent Bank, a most influential establishment, which at a later period than that of which I am speaking, and when few estates were not more or less encumbered, held nearly three-fourths of the mortgages in the colony. Though his official situation in the colony prevented Mr. Montagu from being a Director of the Bank, yet he represented in it, for himself and others, stock to a very large amount, and it was well understood in the colony that the Manager of the Bank, Mr. Swanston, conferred with him on every important occasion, and that the Bank and the Colonial Secretary reflected and augmented each other's influence. The people of Van Diemen's Land are well aware that for years the Derwent Bank has held half the colony in its thraldom.

Having mentioned two leading members of that family compact or party by which I found myself surrounded, and who, from their official situations, were brought into daily and close communication with me, it is not necessary to go at present into further details. The existence of such a party was known to the whole colony; it was recognized by name, in conversation, and in the periodical press; nor was its designation altogether a stranger to the newspapers of England.

I could not but be aware that a party so strongly bound by ties of relationship and of gratitude to my predecessor, and who were powerful instruments in carrying out his measures, might, should a change of policy become necessary, or should any views of my own militate strongly against its prejudices or partialities, become extremely difficult to manage.

At an early period of my government it was not difficult for me to perceive that I was more effectively supported by Mr. Montagu in any measure which carried out the views of the late Lieut.-Governor, than in the efforts I made to conciliate

---

* This fact is stated to show to those who after reading Lord Stanley's Despatch might doubt the correctness of the fact, that the suspension by the Governor even of a Colonial Secretary is not an event of unexampled occurrence.

parties hitherto adverse or obnoxious to the government; but for these indications I made large allowance, in consideration of his long service under Sir George Arthur, whose policy and feelings he had been trained to share, and they were not of a nature to lead to any misunderstanding between us.

Mr. Montagu was zealous in business, extremely active and assiduous, and above all he strove to render himself necessary to me, an object which was much favoured by some circumstances connected with my then private secretary, and which made it exceedingly difficult for me to co-operate with equal cordiality with both parties.

I have ever felt myself bound, to the utmost of my power, to support the officers who served under me, and Mr. Montagu evinced his confidence in this disposition, when, on occasion of his being attacked by a newspaper on some point on which he felt very sensitive, he requested and received my contradictory testimony for transmission to the Secretary of State. And of Mr. Forster I may say that he has repeatedly and candidly acknowledged to me, that whatever popularity he possessed in the colony began with my administration and continued to increase with it.

It may be gathered from all these circumstances, that I appeared, especially in the eyes of those who were opposed to the late administration, to identify myself with it, an impression which was I believe willingly fostered by Mr. Montagu and Mr. Forster, since it added to their personal influence, whilst it enabled them to attribute to some sinister secret influence all those cases in which the assertion of my will was in known opposition to their wishes. I am now throwing the light of after-knowledge and experience on a period in which Mr. Montagu possessed my almost unlimited confidence.

In the first session of the Legislative Council, I threw the doors of the council-room open to the public, having obtained in England the sanction of the Secretary of State to a measure which I felt required due deliberation, as it would almost inevitably involve the adoption of a similar measure in the other Australian colonies; and on the same occasion I took both pride and pleasure in bringing forward, in my Address to the Council, the honourable testimony borne to Sir G. Arthur in reply to a despatch which he had addressed to Lord Glenelg on his recall, and which was contained in a despatch addressed to myself.

The bringing publicly forward this eulogium of my predecessor, instead of quietly depositing it in the archives of my office, was condemned by some as a gratuitous intrusion of a topic not alike acceptable to all, but by, as I conceive, a more right-minded portion of the community it was regarded with approbation. Sir G. Arthur's relatives thanked me for the tribute paid to their late Governor, and that officer himself afterwards conveyed to me, in terms highly flattering to me and honourable to himself, his acknowledgements, not only for this, but for the general consideration evinced towards him in my early conduct of affairs.

Before the next session of the Legislative Council, I had an opportunity of infusing into it a portion of the independent and liberal sentiments of the community, by nominating to a vacant seat a gentleman of great wealth and of superior talents, now deceased, but whose politics were conscientiously opposed to the late Lieutenant-Governor; and in my subsequent appointments it was equally my object to represent as much as possible the interests and sentiments of all the respectable classes of society, and to counteract the too prevailing influence of one family and its partisans.

To every succeeding member of council of whom I had the nomination, I distinctly made known the perfectly independent tenure by which he held his seat; and all will bear witness, that with whatever tenacity I may have urged some measures of my government which I deemed necessary for the public welfare, I have ever respected that independence, and that they have not been the less honoured by me in social life, because of an occasional opposition which tended to frustrate my purposes. By these and similar means, party-spirit became less virulent, and a beneficial change was wrought in the aspect of society.

After a period of about two years, Mr. Montagu obtained from me leave of absence to visit England with his family. It was on some accounts a very inconvenient period for making changes in his department, and I would willingly have induced him to defer his departure; but Mr. Montagu gave me family reasons of such urgency, that they more than balanced in his representation the retention of his office, if the alternative were required.

In granting Mr. Montagu's request, I saw that his presence in England might be of infinite advantage to the colony if he had legitimate access to the Colonial Office, and had means of making available his knowledge and experience in colonial affairs, and especially on the subjects of emigration and convict discipline. The latter was in a state of transition; the old system of assignment being under sentence of condemnation, whilst nothing very definite was yet promulgated as to what should take its place. My despatches on this subject were to go home in the same ship with Mr. Montagu, and I offered them to his perusal beforehand, that he might be the better prepared, if he saw occasion, to explain and support the views they contained.

Mr. Montagu declined reading them at the time on the ground of the great pressure of official business and of his personal affairs, but accepted permission to read them on his voyage. I furnished him also with strong recommendatory letters to the Secretary of State for the Colonies (Lord J. Russell) and to one or two subordinate members of the Colonial Office, besides many others to private friends.

The friendship I had always felt for Mr. Montagu seemed, as is usual in such cases, to augment with the opportunity thus afforded me of obliging him, and this feeling was further confirmed by the intimacy which arose between him and the members of my family, when he was enabled before his departure for England, having disposed of his own residence, to become with his family my guest, for a short period, at Government House. It was either at this, or at a nearly identical period, that he expressed to me his regret at not having before become intimately acquainted with Lady Franklin, accompanying this observation with other remarks, which proved or appeared to prove that that lady had won his entire confidence and esteem; and he gave a farther proof of this by hoping that she would correspond with Mrs. Montagu during absence, and by requesting for himself that she would favour him with her written notes on those subjects on which they had conversed, and which he " felt sure he could make use of in England with great benefit " *.

The subjects chiefly alluded to were the means of education in the colony, and the moral tendencies of the contemplated changes in convict discipline, a subject on which Mrs. Fry had had much conversation with Lady Franklin previous to my departure from England, and on which (particularly on the condition of female convicts) she had requested Lady Franklin's communications.

It will be presently seen why I make these apparently trivial and domestic revelations.

* These terms are used by Mrs. Montagu in a note (still in Lady Franklin's possession) which she wrote at Mr. Montagu's request, to remind Lady Franklin of his wishes on this subject.

There were circumstances attending the temporary vacation by Mr. Montagu of his office and my choice of Mr. Forster, whom he urgently recommended to me, as his *locum tenens*, on which I do not intend here to dwell; suffice it to say, that the appointment of Mr. Forster, which was chiefly grounded on the solemn assurance given me by Mr. Montagu* that he would certainly return to the colony, alienated from me the attachment and deprived me of the zealous and able services of another officer of my government, who conceived he had better claims than Mr. Montagu's brother-in-law to the vacated office, while the preference did not, as it will afterwards appear, secure to me the fidelity of him at whose earnest solicitation I made the decision.

Those who knew Mr. Montagu best were aware before he left Van Diemen's Land that he never intended to return unless he failed in other objects of ambition which occupied his thoughts and efforts during his residence in England, and this fact could not but become apparent to me when I received announcements the most positive, from himself of his return, which were in direct contradiction to the communications made at the same time to his correspondent in the colony Mr. Forster, who was however authorized to inform me that there was little or no probability of the event anticipated. Letters by the same ship and bearing the same date brought these contradictory statements, of which I will say no more than that however desirable Mr. Montagu might have felt it to keep up his credit and influence in the colony by the announcement of his return, in case such an event should at last take place, the mode by which he attempted to effect it was not exactly that which might have been expected from him.

It was apparently in a similar spirit that Mr. Montagu withheld from me, while in England, the result of his communication at the Colonial Office, which he transmitted freely however to Mr. Forster, from whom alone I derived such meagre portions of information on subjects immediately affecting the interests of the colony as were either pointed out by Mr. Montagu himself for communication, or were the result of Mr. Forster's discretion. Some clue to this want of confidence was disclosed when

---

* I gave to the Secretary of State this solemn assurance of Mr. Montagu, as one of my reasons for the appointment of Mr. Forster.

the advice tendered by Mr. Montagu to the Secretary of State on the changes in contemplation in the convict system, appeared in some points to differ considerably from my own. Mr. Montagu alleged however as a reason for his reserve, an illness from which he had been informed I was suffering in Van Diemen's Land. It is strange that Mr. Montagu should have relied so much on the continuance of this illness, as to think it necessary at the distance of ten or twelve months to presume on my unfitness to receive his communications; but be this as it may, Mr. Montagu, on his return to the colony, made this apology, and I felt bound to accept it.

Mr. Montagu was absent from the colony somewhat more than two years. On his return I willingly put aside some unpleasant impressions which the circumstances I have just mentioned had left on my mind, and felt, after some necessary explanations, that the resumption of his duties should be the renewal of our former cordiality.

But Mr. Montagu's pretensions, as they afterwards developed themselves, were not limited to the possession of my confidence, and the sphere, always sufficiently extensive, of his former influence: he aimed at that inversion of our relative positions which Lord Stanley would appear under certain conditions to regard with so much indulgence, as explained by him in the document prefixed to this narrative.

Mr. Montagu had returned, it was understood, with a large increase to his commissions for the Derwent Bank, and with a vast accession of claims to political importance derived from his boasted intimacy with the officers of the Colonial Office in Downing-street.

From this latter position, viewed in connexion with the statement he made of his repeated refusals of places not only of emolument but of power, it could scarcely be doubted that Mr. Montagu's return to the subordinate office of Colonial Secretary in Van Diemen's Land was in his estimation an act of condescension. This sentiment however was veiled from my observation; but I could not but be sensible that Mr. Montagu had become more jealous of control, and that his determination, whenever we differed, was to carry his point at all hazards.

Neither could I any longer resist the impression which had prevailed in the colony before he went to England, though then rejected by me, that his love of influence and power was indulged at my expense, and that he wished it to be believed that in him resided all the energy and power of the government, and that he was desirous of shifting from himself only that share of responsibility which he found inconvenient or unpopular: anything that was unpalatable to indivtduals or disagreeable in its results was willingly attributed to me; popular and pleasant things were all of the procuring of Mr. Montagu.

Nevertheless these manifestations were not immediately, or all at once, developed; they became so by circumstances.

The circumstances which, about six months after Mr. Montagu's return to the colony, led to the complete development of his ambitious policy and to the crisis which followed, were these:—

I had removed from his post of District Surgeon (which includes the medical charge of prisoners within certain limits) a young man who was represented to me as having carelessly and inhumanly neglected his duty in a particular case. The " Principal Medical Officer" (as the Head of the Convict Medical Department is called) recommended that he should be severely reprimanded. The Colonial Secretary, through whom the report came to me, added his recommendation that he should be dismissed. 1 concurred, after examining the papers, in the latter suggestion, and moreover wrote some severe animadversions on the Surgeon's conduct, to the extent of intimating my impression, that had the patient been promptly looked after, his life might possibly have been saved. Subsequent circumstances were brought forward which gave a more favourable aspect to the case. I was moreover made aware that the comment I had written upon it greatly aggravated the Surgeon's offence. It was the opinion both of Mr. Montagu and Mr. Forster that I had inadvertently conveyed a charge of manslaughter against Dr. Coverdale, and Mr. Forster even expressed to me his belief that the Attorney-General's opinion should have been taken as to the tendency of my observations*.

These facts convinced me I had acted with some precipitation, and not having yet learnt that it is a greater blunder in a ruler to repair than to commit an error, it was a relief to my mind

---

* As this commentary and suggestion were not made until some time after the memorandum conveying the imputation had been written by me and acted upon, they could only produce upon me a most painful impression and great anxiety to repair the inadvertence.

when I received a respectful memorial from some of the most respectable inhabitants of the district in question, headed by the very Foreman of the Coroner's Jury, who had previously passed some severe strictures on the Surgeon's conduct, expressing the sense entertained by the neighbours and friends of Dr. Coverdale of his general humanity and skill, and their desire to retain his professional services.

To the revision of my original sentence Mr. Montagu offered the most strenuous opposition. I delayed, at his request, the sending my answer until I had received the memorandum he requested to address to me on the subject; considering that, as one of my official advisers, he had a right freely and fully to express his opinion; but when on receiving it I found his arguments insufficient, and moreover founded in part on mistaken data, I persisted in my decision, of which he was as usual the official organ of conveyance.

It was Mr. Montagu's subsequent conduct which could not be justified or excused.

After absenting himself for several days and sending his papers to me, contrary to his usual custom, without note or comment, I found it necessary to send for him on business which was to be transacted in the Executive Council. Mr. Montagu took the earliest opportunity after this interview to inform me, that he had business also of another nature with me. In a very deliberate and formal manner, he informed me that evil consequences would ensue from the step I had taken respecting Dr. Coverdale; that great excitement prevailed in the district of Richmond; that the petition was an entirely political movement; that he knew how it was "got up"; that Dr. Coverdale's punishment was stated to be *his* (Mr. Montagu's) act, and that to restore him was to degrade his (the Colonial Secretary's) office; that I must not in future expect the same assistance he had hitherto rendered me, though he should keep within the line of his official duty; that he feared however my official labours would be greatly augmented,—he hoped the evil consequences he foresaw might *not* take place. My reply was to the effect, that I hoped also and expected that they would not; that I knew of no agitation whatever in the Richmond district, nor why there should be any; that I neither knew nor cared whether the petition was "got up" by Mr. Gregson as he asserted, or by any one else; that he was at perfect liberty to make known the whole facts of the case; that I saw no reason why his office should be degraded, or his usefulness diminished, or my labours increased; but if that were to be the case, I hoped I should be well able to bear it. My reply might certainly have been couched in less forbearing terms, but hoping that Mr. Montagu was labouring under some delusion, and would soon see the folly and impropriety of these idle and disrespectful observations, I treated the subject as an ebullition of personal feeling of which he would soon himself be ashamed.

Mr. Montagu's however were no idle threats. From that day, or more correctly speaking perhaps, from the day when he reluctantly transmitted my answer to the petition, the current business of my office assumed a very different aspect.

Mr. Montagu absented himself as much as he could from personal attendance; the papers he forwarded to me were no longer accompanied by the necessary information, which had to be elicited step by step from the Colonial Secretary's Office; needless questions were referred to me; every effort was made to overwhelm me if possible with the investigation of minute details, and to make me feel that my dependence on Mr. Montagu's ordinary services was not to be broken with impunity. It was currently reported at this period out-of-doors by Mr. Montagu's nearest adherents, *that he would speedily bring me to terms.* Those who had business to transact at the Colonial Secretary's office reported that they had unusual difficulty in getting any business done.

Another case had grown out of that of Dr. Coverdale, which still farther widened the breach between us*. It left me, after every possible endeavour on Mr. Montagu's part to relieve himself from error at my expense, under the conviction that he had unduly *anticipated* a decision I did actually make in the appointment of a successor to Dr. Coverdale, and had hastened the arrival at Richmond of that successor, with the view, as I could not but conceive, of rendering any revision of my first decision on that case more embarrassing.

This case had not been long disposed of, when my attention was called to the pages of a newspaper, the Van Diemen's Land

* The Kilgour case.

Chronicle, which began to draw invidious comparisons between me and my predecessor Sir George Arthur, and to exhibit myself and my family in odious and malignant characters before the public.

The scurrility of a great portion of the press of Van Diemen's Land is well known, and though there is no denying that it exercises a baneful influence on the community generally, yet are its statements, by the enlightened part of that community, taken for what they are worth.

But the paper in question was ushered into the world with high moral as well as intellectual pretensions, and under peculiar auspices. It contained in its first number, which came out about three months before the agitation of the Coverdale case, the following paragraph : " We shall be enabled to afford our readers the only authentic official information in reference to government measures." In fact, the patronage of this newspaper had been requested of me by Mr. Montagu, and the writers in it were his and Mr. Forster's personal friends. The editor, Mr. Thomas Macdowell, a young man of education and talent, had been recommended to me by a personal friend of my own in England, and, at a period antecedent to the present, had been named to me at Mr. Swanston's instigation, and through Mr. Forster's means, as a fitting person to be made my private secretary,—a suggestion I could not entertain on account of his being then engaged in conducting, in a way not at all suited to my ideas of propriety, the ' Courier ' newspaper.

The brother of this gentleman was the ex-Attorney-General, son-in-law of Mr. Swanston, the Manager of the Derwent Bank, and who was the very intimate friend and associate of Mr. Montagu.

Both the Messrs. Macdowell were at this moment on such terms with me as admitted of the one being a candidate for public employment after resigning the ' Courier ' newspaper, and of the other transmitting to the Secretary of State, through me, his assurances of respectful feeling towards myself, and his desire for renewed official employment in the colony, which owed to my 'unwearied exertions' the blessing of a place of education for his children*.

When Mr. Montagu informed me that Mr. T. Macdowell meant to support the Government, and begged me to allow him a discretionary power to communicate such official intelligence

* Alluding either to the Queen's School, or to the College.

to his paper as it might be thought proper to give, I replied
that I did not think Mr. Macdowell was to be trusted*, and I
asked him also what Mr. Elliston would say to such a thing,
Mr. Elliston being the respectable proprietor of the ' Courier'
newspaper, which had the monopoly of the commissariat tenders
(the greatest boon in the power of the Government to bestow on
any newspaper), and gave a general though uncertain support to
government measures†. It was in allusion to this fact that
Mr. Montagu replied, " Oh! Elliston knows on which side his
bread is buttered." Mr. Montagu farther informed me that
Mr. T. Macdowell had requested him to ask permission to see
Lady Franklin's literary and other periodicals, which he understood were received by her from England. This request I
promised to convey to her‡.

The result of our conversation was, that believing, from Mr.
Montagu's interest in the subject, that Mr. Macdowell would be
in some way or other dependent upon Mr. Montagu, and would
therefore be under control, I acquiesced in the request (though
not in the terms propounded in the first number of the 'Van
Diemen's Land Chronicle'), and expected Mr. Montagu to be
the person to look after its fulfilment. It was entirely foreign
to my habits to attend to these matters, but having Mr. Montagu's conversation fresh in my memory, I repeated the substance
of it to my private secretary in his office §, and again in the presence of other members of my family, including my aide-de-
camp, who perfectly remember its tenour, and shortly after, on
receiving from Count Streleski, a table of the comparative alti-
tudes of the mountains in Van Diemen's Land, desired my
private secretary to forward it to Mr. Macdowell's paper.

* Meaning, to be trusted in the stability of his political sentiments or in the
wielding of his pen, as his sallies in the ' Courier' had already shown.

† Mr. Elliston was unable, in consequence of his pecuniary obligations to
the Derwent Bank, to resist the influence of that establishment, even when it
was exerted against the Government.

‡ Lady Franklin was surprised at the expression, *her* periodicals; and as
she had never patronized any newspaper whatever, and did not wish to begin
now, when especial reference was made to her, she considered it advisable to
take no farther notice of the request, as this would be less disrespectful both
to Mr. Montagu and Mr. Macdowell than a direct refusal. Mr. Montagu was
included in this consideration, since if he had not felt a personal interest in Mr.
Macdowell and his paper, the natural and proper channel for Mr. Macdowell's
request would have been the private secretary or the aide-de-camp.

§ Mr. Henslowe's testimony to this point is amongst the documents which
went home to Lord Stanley, and confirms and remarkably illustrates all I have
stated, besides giving some additional facts.

It appears that Mr. Henslowe, on the faith of the statement I had made to him, that the 'Van Diemen's Land Chronicle' was a paper for which my patronage had been obtained, did himself at different times furnish some articles to it. Their subjects were humorous or critical and wholly unconnected with colonial politics, and the circumstance was unknown to me or to any one else in my household.

It was at a period exactly identical with the public manifestation of a rupture between myself and the Colonial Secretary, which could no longer be concealed, that the insulting articles of the 'Van Diemen's Land Chronicle' arrested the public attention*. Rumours were soon spread abroad in the colony that the Colonial Secretary used the 'Van Diemen's Land Chronicle' directly or indirectly to abuse and degrade the Lieutenant-Governor and his family.

I was myself informed by one who was well-acquainted with Mr. Montagu's mind, that such were the tactics resolved upon; that on a certain day named in advance, the 'Van Diemen's Land Chronicle' would open its fire upon me and boldly espouse Mr. Montagu's cause, and so it happened.

The current impressions on this subject not only reached my private secretary's ears, but were the source of some embarrassment to him; he was repeatedly questioned as to whether the Colonial Secretary continued his countenance and support to the paper,—so much so, as to think it his duty to obtain from Mr. Montagu his unqualified denial to such imputations.

The Colonial Secretary first evaded any direct reply, and then expressed his resentment at the interference. This correspondence took place during a few days that I was absent from the seat of government; it was afterwards laid before me by Mr. Henslowe, and the Colonial Secretary having taken no steps to repudiate the insinuations contained in it, it was impossible for

* Among the papers sent to Lord Stanley is a letter from the Brigade Major, which while it gives evidence of the current reports that Mr. Montagu was in some way or other mixed up with the scurrilous articles in the 'Chronicle,' confirms, on Mr. Montagu's own authority, my assertion of the discretionary power he possessed to give official intelligence, though as he asserts on trivial articles only, a distinction I was by no means aware of. Mr. Montagu has attempted to invalidate this testimony, which has been again persisted in by the Brigade Major. The same document testifies to the intimate companionship existing between Mr. Montagu and Mr. T. Macdowell, and gives an instance of the intimate knowledge Mr. Montagu possessed of the arrangements between the two brothers (Macdowell) as to the production of their several articles.

me any longer to overlook or delay the notice of the very singular position in which Mr. Montagu appeared to have placed himself.

On the 11th of January 1842, I addressed to him a memorandum, reminding him of the conversation which had taken place previous to the appearance of the 'Van Diemen's Land Chronicle,' called his attention to the scurrilous articles against myself and my family which had appeared in it during the last month, and inquired whether he had taken any steps to uphold under such circumstances the dignity of my government.

Mr. Montagu's reply was of a nature which surprised me. Had he disclaimed a knowledge of the offensive articles, I should have thought it extraordinary, since not only were all the colonial papers filed at his office on the day of publication, but Mr. Montagu was himself a subscriber to Mr. Macdowell's paper, and continued to receive it at his house; but such an answer, had it been in Mr. Montagu's power to have made it, would at least have shown that he withheld his countenance of them.

Again, had Mr. Montagu expressed his regret at the offensive articles and at his own inability to control them; had he pointed out that he had abstained from any communication with the editors since the period when it was no longer creditable for him to be connected with them, or had he expressed his anxiety to learn and to execute any wishes of the Lieutenant-Governor on the subject, he would then have done as much perhaps as, in the very unfortunate predicament in which he had placed himself, could have been expected; but Mr. Montagu did not any one of these things.

He informed me that he had no recollection whatever of anything I had said respecting the newspaper, except the conveying a request from the editor for Lady Franklin's periodicals*, and a voluntary communication from myself to him (Mr. Montagu) of Mr. Macdowell's intention to support my government in his newspaper; consequently that it was entirely out of his (Mr. Montagu's) power to "withdraw assistance he had never given," or "to assert the dignity of my government by any step of that description."

Having taken up this position, it must I think be unnecessary for me to prove that Mr. Montagu placed himself in a predica-

---

* Mr. T. Macdowell's letter upon this subject, in answer to one Mr. Montagu addressed to him, says not one word about "Lady Franklin" in reference to the "periodicals."

ment from which I could neither rescue him, nor in which I could suffer him to remain.

In the words of a colonial writer of whose name I am ignorant, but who is evidently not ill-disposed towards Mr. Montagu, " any third-class boy of common capacity must have foreseen that the only result must be (and be so understood by both), that one of the combatants, either the Lieutenant-Governor or himself, must retire from the field*."

The climax of Mr. Montagu's language in the correspondence which passed on this subject was contained in the following insulting imputation in his letter of the 17th of January : " But I trust your excellency will also pardon me for submitting to you,—and I beg to assure you that I do so under a deep conviction of the necessity of supporting my statement,—that while your excellency and all the members of your government have had such frequent opportunities of testing my memory as to have acquired for it the reputation of a remarkably accurate one, your officers have not been without opportunity of learning that your excellency could not always place implicit reliance upon your own."

Unwilling to bandy more words with Mr. Montagu, I paused on the receipt of this letter, and having again patiently reviewed the events of the last few months, and considered the little prospect there was of any real and healthy confidence being re-established between us†, I felt that, without detriment to the public service and dishonour to myself, I could not retain Mr.

---

* Letter of " Civis," Courier. See Appendix A.

† As a proof of the utter and hopeless want of confidence which characterized our relations at this period, I may state that I found it necessary to address a memorandum to Mr. Montagu, dated 18th of January, instructing him to make no use of any conversation which might pass between us, and informing him I should abstain from doing the same myself, in consequence of the experience I had had of the danger of a contrary proceeding.

In ' Murray's Review' of the 4th of February I found it stated, that Mr. Montagu, on the 18th of January, had requested of two public officers then in Government House, and one of whom he detained in it for the purpose, to take down and attest the report of a conversation with myself, with which report he would furnish them, thus providing himself with two witnesses, as he might conceive, against me, in case my statement should differ from his. One of these witnesses was the Colonial Treasurer and the other the Clerk of the Councils ; the latter an officer who is, by the nature of his office, intimately attached to the Lieutenant-Governor.

On reading this fact in ' Murray's Review,' I called upon these officers to give me their statements upon it, and thus found that the newspaper in question had been favoured, though not by either of these gentlemen, with an authentic narrative. I need not remark upon the petty indignity to which a Governor might thus unconsciously have been subjected under his own roof.

Montagu as Colonial Secretary, and accordingly used the powers vested in me of suspending him from office until Her Majesty's pleasure should be known. This determination I conveyed to Mr. Montagu on the 25th of January 1842, exactly three months after his " announcement" of his intention to withhold the assistance he had previously rendered to me as Governor.

On the eve of the day named by himself for handing over the business of his office to his successor, and six days after his suspension had been made known to him, he apologized for the expression above-quoted, which he begged to withdraw, and disavowed any intention of disrespect. I conveyed to Mr. Montagu my appreciation and acceptance of this apology, but as my decision had been formed on public grounds and on the whole of Mr. Montagu's conduct, and was generally known in the community, I could not reverse it for an act of tardy reparation addressed especially to my personal feelings. This act of Mr. Montagu enabled me however to inform him of my intention to recommend him to the Secretary of State for employment as an able and experienced officer, whose services might be useful to the crown in any country but in Van Diemen's Land.

The Secretary of State is well aware how amply I redeemed this pledge, even though I did so under circumstances (intervening between this crisis and Mr. Montagu's departure for England) which might have excused me for renouncing it *.

And the Secretary of State took me at my word,—the despatch at the head of this narrative contains the proof of it. Mr. Montagu was called to the councils of his lordship without delay, for Lord Stanley had need of his services. That those services, which were then deemed of more value than I believe they have since proved themselves to be, should have met with their reward, was a result which might have been expected, but it was not to be expected that the humiliation of Mr. Montagu's late official chief should have entered into the terms by which they were acknowledged.

On the day which immediately followed the communication to Mr. Montagu of my dispensing with his farther services, the

---

* I allude to Mr. Montagu's appeal virtually, though not avowedly, to the public through the newspapers, his threats of unwearied persecution of me and of expulsion from all the clubs of London, and his attempts to excite the popular feeling in his favour at my expense ; for all which extravagances I made more than sufficient allowance in consideration of the excitement of his feelings.

newspapers of that day announced the event in the very words of my communication, though the draft of the memorandum remained locked up in my office; and when that event was finally confirmed and gazetted, the whole of the evening papers on the day following contained, according to the advertisement of the morning papers of that day, an " authentic précis " of the correspondence, including that which had been carried on through my private secretary, between Mr. Montagu and myself, as well as the personal correspondence of those gentlemen, evidently compiled from the documents themselves. This " authentic précis " was an ex-parte statement, full of the grossest misrepresentations.

One of the newspapers alluded to was that of all others which I should have imagined the least likely to have been adopted as a vehicle for authentic communication by any one careful of Mr. Montagu's reputation, being that which is edited by Mr. Robert Lathrop Murray, a person whose reputation is so well known at the Colonial Office, that when I communicated these facts to Lord Stanley, I deemed it quite unnecessary to do more than simply refer to that notoriety. Yet, in spite of these facts, Lord Stanley has " fully exculpated " Mr. Montagu from the imputation " that he made an improper appeal against my suspension of him to the public at large through the local newspapers."

By the same ship which took home Mr. Montagu, who wisely judged that to plead his own cause on the spot was his best policy, I addressed two despatches to the Secretary of State; the first announcing my suspension of Mr. Montagu, and the reasons for it, which are mentioned in a condensed form in the preceding pages, the second entering into the same subject with more detail. Both were accompanied by numerous documents connected therewith, in order that his lordship might be put into full possession of everything which, without violating private confidence and compromising others, could bear upon the case.

The documents were necessarily numerous, since they included not only my own representations, but those which I possessed on Mr. Montagu's side also; but I fear that Lord Stanley, in his very sensitive recollection of the budget, has unconsciously magnified its bulk, since I find him in the margin of No. 150 Despatch, enumerating two which did not relate to Mr. Montagu's suspension, though they treated of a case in which he necessarily made a conspicuous figure*.

* The St. George's Church case.

Lord Stanley's formidable list also includes some which were little more than vehicles for the transmission of papers which at Mr. Montagu's request I had caused to be copied from the records of his office and that of the Clerk of the Council, a labour which obliged me to employ additional clerical assistance for several weeks*. My shoulders are deemed broad enough to bear the Colonial Secretary's heavy contribution as well as my own.

With respect to the case alluded to, the St. George's Church case, as forming the subject of two despatches, which Lord Stanley has enumerated in the list of those relating to Mr. Montagu's suspension, it is so amply explained in the Appendix, in the letter of Mr. Henslowe, my private secretary, to Mr. Young, that I feel myself relieved from the necessity of unfolding it here. I shall simply state, that the treatment of it was required by the remonstrance of a late Director of public works, who had been accused by me of having, without my authority, engaged in very costly improvements of a church, for which I had sanctioned only some necessary and simple alterations †.

When Mr. Montagu left the colony I had commenced the investigation of this matter, in the course of which reference was necessarily made to Mr. Montagu, who stated that he was unable to find the plans of the expensive alterations undertaken, and that he had " never seen " the authority on which Capt. Cheyne had commenced the work.

Within a month after Mr. Montagu had sailed, the plans were found and shown to me for the first time, and collateral evidence was produced in support of an assertion made by Capt. Cheyne, that he had acted upon these plans, under instructions, both verbal and written, given him by Mr. Montagu.

As this case involved the expenditure of a considerable outlay of public money, and the conduct of the dismissed Director of public works, it was a duty incumbent upon me to send it home to the Secretary of State, even though its tendency might be to modify the efficacy of the qualified eulogium I had passed upon

* Mr. Montagu requested me to forward to the Secretary of State copies of all the Minutes of Council, notes and memoranda made by himself during the last quarter of 1841 and up to the middle of January 1842 ; the transmission of these documents forms the subject of three of the despatches enumerated by Lord Stanley.

† The cost to the Government of the alterations sanctioned by me were estimated at 150*l*. ; for the improvements and decorations undertaken without my knowledge, the cost of stone alone at the Government Quarry was estimated at above 2000*l*.

Mr. Montagu's fitness for office, and to make it appear as if my last and crowning charge were the one ounce more upon the camel's back, without which the victim might not yet break down under his lading.

By an exertion of that dexterous ingenuity which characterizes Mr. Montagu's ordinary mode of defence, he, when called upon by Lord Stanley for explanation, involves it in a cloud of detail which mystifies his reader and disappears himself in the vapour he has raised, whilst one solid impression alone remains upon Lord Stanley's mind, that, namely, of my having brought forward another charge against Mr. Montagu which has not the slightest foundation in truth, since Mr. Montagu " has repelled it to " his lordship's " entire satisfaction," and is " entitled," in his lordship's opinion, " to be completely absolved of the fault imputed to him."

It is anticipating the course of events, but not irrelevant to my purpose, if I here state that *I have myself, since my return to England, had the honour of placing in Lord Stanley's hands that very "authority" of Mr. Montagu's, in his own handwriting and signed by himself, which he informed me he " had never even seen."*

Having brought my narrative to this point, I must trespass on my reader's patience while I revert for a few moments to the past, for the sake of bringing forward an episode which is necessary to the further understanding of my story.

It will be felt as that story advances, that however painful the subject, I have no alternative.

In the first interview which I had with Mr. Montagu after Dr. Coverdale's restoration to office, and after he had pointed out to me the disastrous consequences I might expect from that act, Mr. Montagu informed me of a new view of the case, to which he solicited my attention, apologizing that in bringing it forward he should have to mention the name of a lady. My surprise may be conceived when Mr. Montagu proceeded to intimate to me that it was Lady Franklin who had attempted to agitate the Richmond district in Dr. Coverdale's favour; that at any rate her appearance in that district (she had accompanied me on a visit to a respectable settler there, and had been persuaded by me to stay a day behind) was *connected* with the agitation; that if not connected with it, it was *coincident* with it; that if the coincidence was only *accidental*, it was at least *remarkable*.

Through all these phases of expression did Mr. Montagu convey to me his belief that Lady Franklin had been conducting herself in a manner as unbecoming her position as it was opposed to fact.

The only reason Mr. Montagu could give me for his statement respecting Lady Franklin was a letter he had received from Mr. Forster, to the effect that Lady Franklin had, in conversation with him (Mr. Forster) in the Richmond district, mentioned Mr. Montagu's name in connexion with the removal of Dr. Coverdale, as being the supposed cause of it, or one of the causes; and Mr. Forster considered that the interests of the Government were thereby affected*.

I informed Mr. Montagu that I would refer the matter to Lady Franklin, having never myself heard her mention Mr. Montagu's name in any way whatever connected with Dr. Coverdale. The consequence was a correspondence between Lady Franklin and Mr. Montagu, in which Lady Franklin expressed her keen and indignant sense of the injury done her, and referred him to me for the explanation she had given me, and which she thought in the first instance, before denouncing her officially to her husband, he should have requested of herself.

But Mr. Montagu had no desire for this explanation, and finding that the correspondence ended in nothing but mystification on Mr. Montagu's part, Lady Franklin at my request wrote me a statement of all she said and did in the Richmond district, by which it appeared that she had not mentioned Mr. Montagu's name to any one in any form or manner whatever in relation to the Coverdale story, either in the Richmond district or anywhere else,—had never conceived the idea in her own mind of Mr. Montagu's being the cause of my removing Dr. Coverdale from office, nor had heard the observation made by any one else.

* It is worthy of note, that when Mr. Forster wrote the letter from Campbeltown on which Mr. Montagu avowedly based his representation of Lady Franklin's interference, he was with me at Campbeltown in constant official and personal communication, and that on one occasion he reported to me occurrences connected with the Richmond district, and yet not one word did he communicate of the circumstances respecting Lady Franklin's conduct, which in his opinion " affected the interests of the Government." Had they done so in his estimation, and thus involved the public peace, it would have been incumbent upon him, as chief police magistrate, to have made them known to me.

It also appeared that the only persons who ever mentioned Dr. Coverdale's case to her were the two friends at whose house she was staying at Richmond, and that the lady of that house had told her that it was thought possible the whole of the case might not have been placed before me; an opinion which, without knowing anything of this particular transaction, Lady Franklin combated warmly; and that when the same lady intimated to her that the feeling for Dr. Coverdale was so strong that it was contemplated to get up an expression of the public opinion to me for his restoration, Lady Franklin ventured to say she hoped that would not be done, because of the difficulty which she saw must exist against my reversing my decision, and because, if the petition were not granted, the people of Richmond and Dr. Coverdale would be still less contented than before. The exact words used by Lady Franklin, extracted from the letter she wrote to me by my desire, have been placed before Lord Stanley.

This memorandum of Lady Franklin's I placed in the hands of Mr. Montagu, who read it in my presence, and returned it to me without a single word of acknowledgement or any observation whatever.

Had the matter ended here, however destructive Mr. Montagu's proceedings were of all domestic intercourse or social confidence, yet the public need not have had any cognizance of the matter. Mr. Montagu's policy however was of another kind: he at once assumed the attitude of the injured person, and informed my private secretary, whose domestic acquaintance he had never sought before, that Lady Franklin was now the cause that the intercourse he desired between their respective families could not be cultivated, since it was impossible for Mrs. Montagu to "drive up to the door*." He exhibited extensively Lady Franklin's correspondence with him and with Mr. Forster, but without her explanatory memorandum, or any explanation on her part which was necessary for understanding it; re-asserted all that this memorandum contradicted, and exulted in the cloud of mystification by which he had baffled the object she had in view in writing to him, and which was to convince him of his error and bring him to entertain juster views. Mr. Montagu had the field entirely to himself; Lady Franklin was precluded by every sentiment of delicacy and dignity from recrimination; but she was not slow to perceive the use Mr. Montagu was likely to

* The private Secretary and his family were inmates of Government House.

make of this private quarrel to my injury, and determined, at whatever sacrifice to her personal feelings, to seek for a reconciliation. Through the medium of the Colonial Treasurer, Dr. Turnbull, an intimate friend of Mr. Montagu's, as well as a much-esteemed friend of my own, and afterwards through Sir John and Lady Pedder, Lady Franklin endeavoured to procure a renewal of amicable relations with Mr. Montagu. She offered to throw the correspondence on both sides into the fire, or to abandon any particular expression whatever in her own which might have displeased him, and to meet him again as if nothing had happened, and all this, it is to be observed, while under a deep sense of injury; for Lady Franklin was persuaded that Mr. Montagu's object in denouncing her to me was to create distrust in my mind respecting her, and to destroy my confidence not only in her discretion but in her uprightness, by which means a check would be removed which he persuaded himself existed to the increase of his influence.

Lady Franklin's overtures were of no effect; when her concessions were repeated to Mr. Montagu, he replied (to Dr. Turnbull) that he did not ask for her concessions, and that he believed she was at that very moment dictating some of the correspondence which was going on between him and "Sir John Franklin," on the Kilgour case*.

With respect to the mediation undertaken by Sir John Pedder, it entirely failed, in consequence of the terms in which Mr. Montagu expressed his acquiescence being such as the Chief Justice deemed inadmissible.

These negotiations terminated thus unfavourably on or about the 20th of November, that is to say, within a month of the day on which Mr. Montagu had denounced Lady Franklin to me as the agitator of the Richmond district. It is necessary that these dates should be borne in remembrance.

It was after these proceedings that the 'Van Diemen's Land Chronicle' began those personal and insulting diatribes to which I have already alluded. From the beginning of December 1841 to February 1842, the public read in the leading articles of this weekly journal a series of dastardly and impudent, though cun-

---

* Distressed at this imputation, Lady Franklin condescended to request that Mr. Montagu might be set right on this point. I say *condescended,* because no other word applies fitly to the voluntary denial of a gratuitous and utterly unfounded assertion.

ningly devised falsehoods, the general object of which was to excite hatred and contempt for my government and myself, and the special one, subservient and tributary to the other, to show that Lady Franklin's malign influence over me was the sole cause of Mr. Montagu's suspension, which arose out of her interference in the Coverdale case.

That *fons mali*, the Coverdale case, now for the first time appeared in the public journals; the transactions to which it related had for some time been set at rest; the agitation which Mr. Montagu's imagination had conjured up had not been heard of, and but for the labours of the 'Van Diemen's Land Chronicle,' the "Richmond petition" had slept for ever in the tomb of the Capulets. But its disinterment was required, and it came forth again at the bidding of Mr. Macdowell, to witness to the truth of his reckless assertions. It was in vain that the real and sole author, as the Rev. Mr. Aislabie declared himself to be, of that petition addressed a letter to Mr. Montagu, whom he confounded with the author of the "authentic précis" of the case of Mr. Montagu's suspension published in the 'Courier' newspaper, remonstrating against the use of Lady Franklin's name in connexion with that petition, and claiming exclusive property in it. Mr. Montagu, personating as it would seem the author of the "précis," quoted Lady Franklin against herself, assured Mr. Aislabie he had read in her own handwriting that she was the getter-up of the petition, and pointed out to him that this story was quite consistent with his own. The 'Van Diemen's Land Chronicle' supported Mr. Montagu, and dismissed Mr. Aislabie with gibes and sneers. There was no farther attempt at contradiction*, and the newspaper-reading public must have

* The 'Courier' still occasionally admitted into its columns an article sent to it by individuals it did not desire to offend, but was becoming every day less able to resist the influence of the Derwent Bank. The 'Advertiser' newspaper was changing hands, and had not yet taken up that independent support of the Government which afterwards distinguished it. 'Murray's Review,' the unflinching champion of every monument and relic of the late administration, of which at an earlier period it had been the unscrupulous reviler, was of course the advocate of Mr. Montagu. Its pages were particularly distinguished by their exhibition of passages from the correspondence of Lady Franklin and Messrs. Montagu and Forster, for the benefit apparently of that portion of the public which had not yet been favoured with a sight of it in manuscript. A newspaper which has just come in my way enables me to let Mr. Murray speak for himself as to his possession of authentic information:—
'Murray's Review,' November 18, 1842.—" When Captain Montagu was removed from his office, we published the *whole correspondence* which had taken place; the letter (autograph, of Sir John Franklin) in which that re-

perceived that the Coverdale case was most satisfactorily disposed of.

It is difficult to conceive how, in the absence of all opposition, the rancour could have been sustained which disgraced these unmanly productions, and by what process it was that the ex-Attorney-General, Mr. Macdowell, whose treatment by me in the circumstances which had deprived the colony of his services had been the subject of his eulogium for its fairness, and whose expressions of gratitude for kindness received from me had been transmitted to the Secretary of State*, should have been so suddenly converted into an enemy, and his brother, the hitherto warm and graceful eulogist of Lady Franklin whenever an opportunity presented itself of being so, into her unscrupulous calumniator.

Yet, whatever may have been the impulses under which these gentlemen wrote, no one who knows the connexion then subsisting between Mr. Montagu and Mr. Swanston, the head of the Derwent Bank, and the dependence of the elder Mr. Macdowell on his father-in-law, Mr. Swanston, but must be aware that any offensive writings of theirs, as far at least as the elder Mr. Macdowell was concerned, could have been checked at either of those gentlemen's pleasure.

Instead of this however, Mr. Montagu's intimacy with the editors of the ' Chronicle' was such as to countenance the belief that it met with his approbation. I do not speak of family intercourse, but of that association which the public could best appreciate, because they witnessed it. The elder Mr. Macdowell was constantly to be found in Mr. Forster's office, and Mr. Forster and Mr. Montagu, who until within a few weeks of Mr. Montagu's departure formed one family, living in the same house and receiving their mutual or separate guests at the same table, could not but be confounded in the estimate formed of their private feelings.

When Mr. Montagu and Mr. Forster simultaneously requested of me leave of absence (as they had also done on a former occasion, immediately after the settlement of the Cover-

moval was finally announced we also gave, and we refer the whole colony thereto, whereby the utter falsehood of the statement is made apparent, that *insulting communications to Lady Franklin'* formed any portion of the immediate cause of Captain Montagu's dismissal; further we will not permit ourselves to go."

* See Appendix B.

dale case) in order to go into the interior, Mr. Thomas Macdowell, the avowed editor of the ' Van Diemen's Land Chronicle,' met them by appointment at the house of Mr. Forster's brother at Hamilton, in order to form a third in the party. They travelled together, were seen in the same settlers' houses, bespoke their social fare and accommodations at the same inn, and ended by appearing together as companions at a public sale of stock numerously attended, at no great distance from Hobart Town.

Mr. Montagu has denied to Lord Stanley any association or influence whatever with the abusive newspapers or their authors; I must leave him to reconcile these statements with the internal evidence of the newspapers themselves and with the fact I have just related, or with the additional fact that the elder Mr. Macdowell, the ex-Attorney-General, formed one of the members of the last family-party at Mr. Forster's house on the day of Mr. Montagu's embarkation.

My reader will look back to Lord Stanley's despatch, and consider the opposite conclusion to which his lordship has come upon this subject. Lord Stanley's exculpation of Mr. Montagu exhausts the power of language to make it more complete; and this is an inevitable conclusion, because his lordship's sentiments on the conduct of a public officer who has any connexion, direct or indirect, with the public press for the purpose of embarrassing the government under which he serves, are such as would not permit him the exercise of the smallest indulgence*.

But I must hasten to the conclusion, which will probably prove to the reader an unexpected one, of the episode I commenced a few pages back.

On the 27th of January 1842, two days after Mr. Montagu's suspension had been communicated to him, but before he had actually resigned his office into the hands of his successor, Dr.

---

* In making the above observations, I have not been unmindful of a fact which Mr. Montagu has had ready in his own defence, viz. that the ' Van Diemen's Land Chronicle,' previous to its outbreak against me, contained one or more articles highly condemnatory of Mr. Montagu with reference to Captain Cheyne's removal from office, and admitted into its pages the whole of the official correspondence between those two officers on the Bridgewater case.

The secret history of this circumstance is unknown to me; but if it prove, as it would appear to do, that the editor of the newspaper had at one time a quarrel with the Colonial Secretary, it only brings out with the greater force the unscrupulous adherence which he afterwards manifested to Mr. Montagu when it was thought desirable to exhibit the tactics which would be opposed to me. (See page 19.)

Turnbull requested an interview with Lady Franklin; his object was to request, on Mr. Montagu's part, her intercession with me for a reconciliation. Dr. Turnbull was commissioned to say that Mr. Montagu was ready to apologize in the fullest manner, consistently with his feelings as a gentleman, for everything that had given me displeasure; that he would pledge himself to carry out all my views for the future with the utmost zeal, even on points on which he might continue to differ with me in opinion; that having been already suspended, he should regard it (his restoration to office) as entirely " an act of grace." He requested Lady Franklin's mediation and good offices. No reference appears to have been made by Mr. Montagu, since none was communicated to Lady Franklin, to recent misunderstandings and rejected offers of reconciliation on her part; she felt that it was because she had been injured by Mr. Montagu that he had now chosen her for his advocate, and such an appeal has ever been with generous minds irresistible.

Yet Lady Franklin had too clear a notion of my relative position with Mr. Montagu at this juncture, and too correct an one of her own, not to feel the difficulty of the predicament in which she was placed. She promised Dr. Turnbull her efforts to incline me to listen to Mr. Montagu's wishes, but gave him little hope of success, since she anticipated the greatest objection on my part to her interference. And Lady Franklin's anticipations were fully justified, for I entirely disapproved of her being made a channel of communication, and so informed Dr. Turnbull. Notwithstanding, the negotiation was not entirely abandoned; Lady Franklin gave into my hands some papers which had been sent to her by Mr. Montagu, drawn from the records of the Colonial Office, the object of which was to seek further to engage her sympathy with his feelings, by proving that he had once in Downing-street spoken of me as " an absent friend"*. On the appearance the next day of an abusive article in the ' Van Die-

---

* The subject of these papers is unimportant, but they included a correspondence between Mr. Stephen, the Under Secretary of State, and Mr. Montagu, which contains the expression alluded to.

The papers had not been returned to Mr. Montagu when, after he had quitted his office and before his embarkation (that is, on some day between the 2nd and 10th of February), he wrote to Dr. Turnbull to beg him to send them back, designating them as the " Loane Papers." It is remarkable that Mr. Montagu's note was either ante-dated or post-dated a month. Notwithstanding, if still in Dr. Turnbull's possession, it remains as a record of the active steps taken by Mr. Montagu to engage Lady Franklin's good offices.

men's Land Chronicle,' Mr. Montagu sent to me to express his regret at it, and his sense of the injury it must do to himself, and in the presence of several witnesses in the street he upbraided Mr. T. Macdowell with his abuse of a lady; finally, on the evening of the day when his successor was to relieve him in his office, I received from him that apologetic letter to which I have already alluded, and on the frankness and earnestness of which Lord Stanley has commented. There is no denying these characteristics of Mr. Montagu's letter of the 31st of January, and I am not ashamed to say that it deeply affected me, even though I had a light by which to judge of it which Lord Stanley did not possess, and which took away from the spontaneous and disinterested character which Mr. Montagu attempted to give it after it had failed in its object.

Mr. Montagu's letter of the 31st January is an anomaly in his correspondence with me. He acknowledges the announcement he made to me of his intention to withdraw from cordial co-operation, is able to understand at once all those observations on my part which had hitherto baffled all his efforts to comprehend them, and begs to offer me every reparation and apology for the offensive imputation he had made in a former communication.

I regarded this letter as a last effort of Mr. Montagu or his friends to procure his reinstatement in office; and though my deep and anxious deliberations on it did not result in my yielding to his desire, which it appeared to me neither safe nor consistent to do, yet was it not altogether written in vain, since it enabled me to put more warmth into the terms by which I sought to avert from Mr. Montagu any permanently serious consequences either to his reputation or his pecuniary interests from the step I had taken. My forbearance and consideration in this instance have I believe been used against me. The eulogium I passed upon Mr. Montagu's talents may have been used as an argument why I should not have deprived myself of them, and my recommendation of him to office in any other colony than Van Diemen's Land as the reparation offered by an uneasy conscience for the infliction of a gratuitous wrong. Be it so. I may stand convicted of a political blunder, but retain the blessed consciousness of having done no man, not even Mr. Montagu, more injury than the stern demands of duty forced upon me.

It does not appear to me necessary to enter into any detail of

D

the manner in which Lady Franklin executed the commission with which Mr. Montagu entrusted her. Those who know her will be assured she acted feelingly and faithfully; and if there be any who have accepted Mr. Montagu's representations of her as exhibited in the ' Van Diemen's Land Chronicle' and its plagiarists, or in the pages of Mr. Montagu's manuscript book, to them I feel myself released from affording explanations which perhaps nothing I could say would render acceptable.

Previous to embarking for England, Mr. Montagu, under the influence I presume of some compunction as to the policy he was about to pursue in conducting his defence in England, inquired of Dr. Turnbull whether he believed Lady Franklin was sincere in the mediation she had undertaken. " As sincere as it is possible to be," replied Dr. Turnbull. Mr. Montagu returned no answer, and embarked without conveying a word of notice or acknowledgement to Lady Franklin.

When Dr. Turnbull mentioned these circumstances to Lady Franklin, she replied, that she could not be blind to the policy which Mr. Montagu had in view respecting her, and that she believed a conspiracy was organized which would have its agents here (in the colony) as well as its prime agent at home, for the purpose of ruining her husband, if they could do so, through her. Lady Franklin excused herself for entertaining a conception which involved a belief of so much falsehood and want of principle in the agents, by referring to private letters, which detailed how actively this policy was already pursued by Mr. Montagu's relations and friends in the colony, and by pointing to the actual state of the local press, and particularly to the pages of the ' Van Diemen's Land Chronicle' and the ' Courier,' which appeared now to be printed and published for no other purpose than to advocate the policy supposed. Dr. Turnbull endeavoured to combat this conviction of Lady Franklin, as arguing a dereliction of principle in Mr. Montagu of which he did not believe him capable, adding however, " if after what has passed, he (Mr. Montagu) ever does use your name in any other language than that of respect and gratitude, I will say it will be the basest of actions."

At this period one of the editors of the local press, by way apparently of apology to my private secretary for the articles he admitted into his columns, described the power which Mr. Montagu wielded as " tremendous"; indeed the " authentic précis" which had been sent to the 'Courier,' and which gave Mr. Montagu's own version of his suspension, had been received by that paper upon authority which it could not dispute. The press was at this period an engine to influence the public mind for a special private purpose. The most startling leading articles were written expressly for Lord Stanley's eye (having first served their purpose in the colony), in order to make him believe that statements so uncompromising and so bold must needs be true and indisputable, or else the public would not bear them*. The Tasmanian editors have, I am sorry to say, an overweening confidence in the curiosity and credulity of successive Secretaries of State for the Colonies, and issue forth their most *telling* articles on the eve of departure of the latest despatch-bag, fondly trusting that the freshest newspaper at least will be placed before the Minister and attract his attention. This practice is well understood in the colony and boasted of.

With the strong suspicion I had on my mind that Mr. Montagu's intended policy in conducting his defence at the Colonial Office would be to show that the offence he had committed

---

* There are some things the public will not bear. When the editor of the ' Review' got possession, after my departure from Van Diemen's Land, of a *stolen* private journal of the Rev. J. P. Gell, written while he was still an inmate of my family on his first arrival in the colony, and when that receiver of stolen goods picked out the most piquant and personal passages of this private journal, strung them together by asterisks and published them in the columns of his newspaper, in order to give to the public an epitome of the confidential conversations and domestic manners of Government House, of which he promised them further supplies, the weight of a whole community's reprobation fell on the hoary head of that editor.

I am not aware of more than one Tasmanian journal (though my acquaintance at present with the productions of the Tasmanian press is very limited) that was found to transfer the guilty columns of the ' Review' to its own pages.

The ' Launceston Examiner,' in a long and creditable article upon this transaction, has the following observation :—

" But if the plan of the ' Review' is correct, then we must advertise for private correspondence and personal memoranda ; we must advise the valets of gentlemen to ransack their employers' cabinets ; and having secured the secrets of the *escritoire*, pass them through the auctioneer's hands, purchase them in a lot of useless pamphlets, and publish the intelligence obtained, in juxtaposition with a pious expression of horror at the personality of the press."—*Launceston Examiner*, February 28th, 1844.

Mr. Gell endeavoured in vain to recover his journal, and thus was unable even to verify the passages said to be extracted from it.

I may remark that some key to the personal malignity of the editor of the ' Review' towards myself and my family may be found in the fact, that when, several years before I left Van Diemen's Land, he had the assurance to send in his card to the aide-de-camp, preparatory to a levee I was about to hold, I desired it might be *returned* to him.

against Lady Franklin, by denouncing her as an agitator and exciter of discontent, was the real cause of his suspension, there seemed to be but one course for me to pursue, but this was a painful one; and indeed it was not until after much anxious deliberation that I introduced into an official despatch the name of a lady, though that lady could look to me alone for protection from calumny and insult. In so doing I limited my observations to the mere dry statement that Mr. Montagu had imputed to Lady Franklin a desire and attempt to agitate the Richmond district in favour of Dr. Coverdale, that the real facts of that case were subversive of this statement, and had been the means of exposing her to unwarrantable publicity, accompanying this very succinct account with the letter which Mr. Aislabie addressed to Mr. Montagu on reading the " authentic précis" in the ' Courier' (see p. 29), the latter's reply, and an extract in refutation of that reply from the very letter or memorandum of Lady Franklin to which Mr. Montagu referred as evidence against her, and which he had read in my presence. I did not think proper to trouble his lordship with any notice of the private communications which had passed between Mr. Montagu and Lady Franklin relative to this affair, and with respect to Mr. Montagu's last critical act, that of his application to Lady Franklin for her intercession,—a secret which he had himself hidden, and which he desired Dr. Turnbull to hide from his nearest relations and friends,—I abstained from placing it unnecessarily before his lordship. Mr. Montagu's subsequent conduct has since forced upon me a disclosure which he must be well aware I could have used from the first with great advantage, and which he could not have attempted to invalidate, since the very secrecy which he observed prevented his supporting his own statements by a single witness, whilst on the other side there were three witnesses to attest the same facts, besides those members of my family to whom Lady Franklin had Dr. Turnbull's permission to communicate it.

The specific grounds on which I had removed Mr. Montagu from office during Her Majesty's pleasure having been detailed in the two despatches I have already mentioned, p. 23, I wrote a supplementary one, dated the 18th February 1842, the object of which was twofold: viz. first, to explain as well as I could in a document of this nature, and with means limited by the checks which my respect for my predecessor and my desire not unnecessarily to injure Mr. Montagu or any one connected with him, multiplied around me, the general reasons why my present estimation of Mr. Montagu, and of the value of his services, differed from that I had once entertained; and secondly, to prove that under no circumstances of change in the officer administering the government ought Mr. Montagu to be restored to office in Van Diemen's Land. The reasons by which I supported this latter position were such as I deemed no minister, with Lord Stanley's high responsibilities, and who possessed his devoted zeal for the welfare of the colonies he governed, would consider himself justified in disregarding; and thus, when his lordship informed me in his despatch No. 150, that he considered it highly inexpedient to restore Mr. Montagu to his office in Van Diemen's Land, I believed, that however inconsistent was the declaration with the tone of his lordship's despatch, yet at least his lordship had respected this, my conscientious and solemn statement.

In the same despatch, I alluded to several cases of misunderstandings between public officers and the Government, or with one another, which had, in more than one instance, obliged me to dispense with the services of individuals who perhaps, under less adverse circumstances than those in which they were placed, might still have served the Government with alacrity and zeal. It is not my intention to shift from myself the responsibility of these painful duties, or to exonerate any public servant from blame, by the provocations to which personal hostility, or ill-will, or intrigue, in the individual who formed the channel of communication with the Government, may have subjected him, but certain it is, that to such sinister influences have these officers almost invariably attributed the results of their indiscretions. This observation is not irrelevant or gratuitous when referring to Mr. Montagu, since it is well known that one of the points which he worked most unscrupulously and successfully with Lord Stanley against me, was that of the cases here alluded to. I say unscrupulously, because the suspension of the Director of Public Works in the year 1841 was urged upon me by Mr. Montagu on public grounds, as a measure which admitted of no delay*; and on a previous occasion, when the permission was

* Mr. Montagu once ventured to hint at his own resignation being the alternative of Captain Cheyne's retention, but afterwards voluntarily retracted

given me to remove a public officer who had offered an opposition alike vigorous and unbecoming, to a measure of my government*, which I had resolved, from a sense of its importance to the public interests, if possible, to carry, Mr. Montagu, then in England, and profiting by the access he had to the Colonial Office to convey to me such information as he thought useful, caused me to be informed, through his confidant and correspondent Mr. Forster, that my delay in effecting this removal had been disapproved of, and in short that if I did not now exercise the power vested in me to remove him, my own "days were numbered."

This is not the place for me to discuss or defend any acts of my government which are not connected with the immediate subject of my present narrative; those to which I now allude need not my justification, since they have been approved of and confirmed by the Secretary of State; but I wish to point out the influences to which Lord Stanley would appear to have submitted his judgement, and also to show that I had substantial reason for entertaining the belief which I expressed to his lordship upon Mr. Montagu's suspension, that henceforth there would be no occasion for any such decisive measures, and that mutual confidence and co-operation might be reckoned upon amongst all the members of my government.

The experience of the last year and a half of my administration of affairs in Van Diemen's Land, viz. from Mr. Montagu's departure till the arrival of my successor, fully justified this anticipation. My government was not weakened, but more firmly united and strengthened by the removal of Mr. Montagu; and if there were a few who identified themselves with him, although their duty should rather have led them, at all hazards, to identify themselves with the Lieutenant-Governor, others, who to their credit, sympathized more with Mr. Montagu in his misfortune than they had ever done with the Colonial Secretary

his words, though he ventured to submit to me this proposition,—"that as in the usual course of things my administration must be drawing to a close ('though of course if I wished it I could remain as long as I pleased'), it would be an unfair and a cruel thing to leave to a new Governor the task of commencing his government by removing a public officer with whom it was impossible to act, and whose removal was my own duty." Mr. Montagu's words may have been more guarded than these, but I am faithful to the sense.

* This case being that of a government officer does not offer any contradiction to the statement I have made, p. 10.

in his pride of place and influence, and many who deemed they could not safely express any opinion but such as they were solicited or expected to express*, though the public generally were ignorant of any other version of affairs than that which Mr. Montagu and his own party newspapers had given them, uncontradicted, yet I will venture to say that the removal of Mr. Montagu was a popular, as well as a necessary measure; that it met with the approval of the great body of the colonists, and that many regretted only that for the peace of the colony, that which had been done then had not been done before. This sentiment came to me from many quarters, accompanied by expressions of respect and attachment and of confidence in my government, which were both seasonable and gratifying to me.

The productions of a corrupt and mendacious portion of the press, inasmuch as they were addressed to the worst passions and weaknesses of the community, had fallen far short of their object, and though written with the ulterior view of conveying instruction and advice to the Secretary of State, had not yet obtained his countenance.

After the embarkation of Mr. Montagu, on the 10th of February 1842, if tranquillity were not at once restored, yet the heaving of the waters was only the remains of the storm that was passing away. Even party-spirit was constrained to suppress its manifestations and to wait for a future day, when perhaps the thunder-cloud might return. The 'Van Diemen's Land Chronicle' itself, after a few more scurrilous articles, which lasted as long as the supposed transmission of my last despatches to England on the one absorbing subject, showed symptoms of exhaustion. It struggled on however two or three months longer, lived to congratulate me facetiously on my return from an exploring expedition to Macquarie Harbour, and then died what may indeed be called a *natural* death, though neither full of years nor of honour, since it had apparently accomplished all the ends of its existence.

I took advantage of the profound tranquillity which succeeded

* It was never lost sight of that Mr. Montagu might *return,* and his best friends will scarcely deny that he has a vindictive memory. It was even rumoured that he might *return as my successor,* and certain it is that Mr. Montagu did his best to favour such an impression, and openly spoke of this prospective event after he had left the colony.

the departure of Mr. Montagu, and the thorough confidence I placed in the long-tried and worthy officer* who succeeded him, to accomplish an expedition, which, whenever undertaken, must have involved an absence of several weeks from official quarters, and an entire interruption of communication during the greatest portion of that period. The object of this expedition was to visit the abandoned penal settlement of Macquarie Harbour on the western coast of Van Diemen's Land, with the view of ascertaining whether the capabilities of that place were such as to make it desirable to re-establish a penal station there for the reception of the doubly-convicted felons who were now for the first time to be sent to my charge from New South Wales and Norfolk Island. Macquarie Harbour had hitherto been accessible only by sea, and was of difficult entrance; the interruptions to communication with it were frequent, and were amongst the reasons which had caused the abandonment of the settlement by my predecessor, after much labour and expense had been bestowed on its formation. It was a part of my plan therefore to examine into the nature of the country between it and the settled districts, in order that I might judge of the fitness of employing a large body of convicts to establish a land-communication between them, and of opening the country to the occupation of enterprising settlers. I had, at a period long antecedent to the present, announced my intentions on this subject to the Secretary of State, but had hitherto been prevented from carrying them into execution.

As a preliminary step for the furtherance of my project at the present moment, a small gang of from eight to ten convicts had been employed for several months in setting up marks, and in cutting a foot-track through the hitherto impenetrable forests in which in former years many a wretched fugitive from the penal settlement had perished. This party was increased, when I was able myself to commence the journey, by an additional number of prisoners, to carry tents, tools, and provisions. The prisoners were selected for their good conduct, and for being within a short period, according to the then existing rules of convict discipline, eligible for indulgence or alleviation of their sentences,—circumstances which it is not unimportant for me to notice here in reference to a future part of my narrative. The history of this

* Mr. Boyes, Colonial Auditor.

little expedition, however interesting to the parties concerned in it, is not subject-matter for these pages. The sudden breaking-up of the weather, after I had already advanced into the unsettled districts, and the prevalence of contrary winds, which made me a prisoner in Macquarie Harbour, prolonged my return much beyond the period anticipated when I set off, and caused some uneasiness respecting us in the community,—a circumstance to which I attribute in a great degree the cordiality and warmth with which my return was greeted by all classes.

The untoward delay alluded to was not without some good results, since it enabled me to give my mind to the consideration of a subject, which, but for the increase of labour that had been thrown upon me by the conduct of the late Colonial Secretary, would have earlier engaged my active attention.

The assignment of convicts into private service, which had till lately been the condition of prisoners on their first arrival in the colony, was abolished, and instructions had been received and were acted on, to dispose of the newly-arrived prisoners in labour-gangs, under the control and in the service of the Go-vernment, in different parts of the country. This new system was however to apply only to a small portion of the period which assignment used to occupy, and I had hitherto received no instructions as to what was to be done with the prisoners when that small portion of the period expired. My despatch to the Secretary of State of the 1st of April 1842, written during my absence on the exploring expedition, contained some sug-gestions on this head, and an intimation of my intention to give it maturer consideration, and to act upon my own responsibility if instructions should continue to be withheld. On my return to head-quarters my attention was attracted still more forcibly to the necessity of taking upon myself such a responsibility, having before my eye the practical evils of prolonging the first stage of punishment in the case of prisoners who were eligible for a second; and I was still further impressed with the convic-tion that the administration of the department required some amendment.

It is here necessary to observe, that about a year before the period of which I am now speaking, I had, on the urgent repre-sentations of the Colonial Secretary and of the Chief Police Magistrate (Messrs. Montagu and Forster), formed the superintendence of the government gangs into a new department, under the name of the " Probation Department," and placed it under the control of Mr. Forster, who thus became Director of the Probation Department, in addition to his former office of Chief Police Magistrate. He and Mr. Montagu saw great advantages for the public service in this union, which I considered it was worth while to prove; whilst at the same time it was distinctly anticipated and stipulated by me, that its duration was uncertain.

The experience of a twelvemonth which had now elapsed, convinced me of the necessity for a separation of the offices thus united in the person of Mr. Forster. I found that the gangs dispersed all over the country, and which were increasing with unusual rapidity, required closer attention than it was possible for the Chief Police Magistrate, who was also an Executive Councillor, with all his energy to give to them; and if this was apparent when the business of the Probation Department was confined merely to that first stage of the prisoners' punishment to which I have alluded, it was evident that when it came to include the multifarious arrangements attendant upon the ulterior condition of the prisoner in his subsequent stages, which I was now about for the first time to introduce, the superintendence of the whole by one individual was a moral and physical impossibility. On the 17th of August therefore I communicated to Mr. Forster my views and decisions upon this subject, but did not bring them into operation, nor relieve Mr. Forster of his charge of the Probation Department, until the 27th of September. He remained after the separation precisely in the same position as he was the year before, when I gave him the superadded charge with its emoluments.

In the organization of the new or developed department, I was much assisted by an able individual* who had long been an esteemed officer of the Van Diemen's Land Company's Establishment, and in that capacity had had considerable experience in the management of convicts. I appointed this gentleman, who had recently quitted the service of the company, to the superintendence of the new department, to which I gave the name of " Department of Convict Discipline," because it was to embrace the whole sequence of transitions and regulations in the convict's life, and appeared to me a name more significant and less

* Mr. Milligan.

liable to misapprehension than that of probation, originally applicable only to the first stage of punishment, and which experience had taught me had been productive among the convicts of mischief.

For the assistance of the head of this new or revised department, in that branch of it which related to the investigation of applicants' claims for servants, I formed a board, including two other officers of my government of great experience and ability* in convict matters; and thus the services of three most efficient individuals were secured for one branch of the department in which I considered a divided responsibility was desirable, in lieu of the divided services of *one*, and this at a cost not exceeding by more than £200 a year the expenses of the late arrangement. The saving which I calculated upon as the consequence of withdrawing the men from the gangs, and enabling them to enter private service on wages, was from £30,000 to £40,000 a year.

My despatch to Lord Stanley in explanation of these changes bears date the 17th of November 1842, when I was enabled to speak with confidence of their early results, and it was accompanied by a "report" of the whole system of convict management in operation. But previously to sending home this elaborate statement, and antecedently even to my communication to Mr. Forster, I wrote a short despatch to the Secretary of State, to *announce* the changes contemplated, which I informed his lordship I should afterwards explain. I must beg the reader, whose memory has been already somewhat taxed, to bear the latter circumstance in remembrance.

Mr. Forster, in his reply to my letter to him of the 17th of August, requested me to submit to Lord Stanley, along with my own, his representations and reports on the department from which he was relieved. With this request, as Mr. Forster well knew, I was bound to comply. There was no other *legitimate* mode in which he could transmit the representations which he was entitled, if he thought proper, to make. Accordingly, when the 'Matilda' sailed on September the 6th, Mr. Forster, still in occupation of his double office, applied to my private secretary to know whether or not my despatches went by that ship, and was informed in the negative, my plans for the new department

---

* Mr. Price, Police Magistrate of Hobart Town, and Mr. Gunn, Superintendent of the Male Penitentiary.

not being yet finally arranged, and my time being much occupied by the business of the Legislative Council then sitting. The inference in my mind from Mr. Forster's application was inevitable, that his own communications for the Secretary of State were delayed until mine were ready, which was not, as I have said, until the 17th of November. The ship conveying these despatches had been long detained in the harbour, and afterwards made a very long passage; but even could I have foreseen these circumstances, I should probably have deemed them of no material importance, since I had already given Lord Stanley notice of the intended changes, and had shown the importance I attached to that communication by sending a duplicate "viâ Bombay," which preceded the arrival in England of the original.

In my despatch of the 17th of November, I had the honour of informing Lord Stanley, that having thus, on my own responsibility and in the absence of instructions from home, remodelled the whole system of convict discipline in the colony as respected male prisoners, I should before long report to him upon the condition of the female convicts, having been for some time making the most searching investigations into the evils of the then existing system.

The changes already effected were referred to in my address to the Legislative Council at this period. The business of this session was carried on with unexampled ease and harmony. I am unable to refer to any former occasion of the kind when the proposed appropriation of the revenue passed the Council with equal facility, and when a better temper or greater unanimity prevailed. It was impossible for me not to feel that public confidence in my government had increased and was increasing, and that the spirit of faction was overruled by the good sense and good feelings of the community.

I refer with the more satisfaction to the period of my government intervening between Mr. Montagu's departure and the close of the year 1842, because I believe it will lose nothing by a comparison with those earlier periods of my administration, which, if any confidence be due to Mr. Montagu's *voluntary communications* to me both on his return from England and during his residence there, had secured the satisfaction and approbation of Her Majesty's Government.

This period of tranquillity and peace was however drawing to a close.

I took little note of the rumours that were afloat on the return of the first ships from England after Mr. Montagu's arrival there, having myself received communications from various quarters, which though not officially derived from Downing-street, left me in no doubt that Lord Stanley approved my act of suspension. Letters from various friends in England congratulated me on this decision, and on the support which Lord Stanley had so justly given to my government. These communications were founded it appears upon assurances which had been given at the Colonial Office, that it was Lord Stanley's determination to retain me in the government, and undoubtedly the conclusion, though illusory, was a natural one.

I make this observation with some reluctance; as without explanation it may appear to indicate an undue anxiety as to my own position, if not the employment by me of those private means of interference with the course of public matters which I am about to expose, as having been so freely employed in the case of my opponents. I must therefore state distinctly, that when I sent home my despatches respecting Mr. Montagu, I left them to their merits and their fate; nor did I, nor did any one belonging to me, ask of a friend to ascertain even so much as what that fate might be at the Colonial Office; still less did it enter into my contemplation to set to work any means which should procure for me a partial or more favourable hearing than the merits of the case demanded. I was too confident of the propriety of my decision in the case of Mr. Montagu to be very solicitous as to its consequences, at least as respected myself; I wish to speak however without disrespect or presumption, my only real care having been to destroy the tyranny and mischievous influence throughout the colony of an individual and a party, who had shown themselves as capable when offended of virulent and vindictive opposition to the government, as under other circumstances they could be zealous in its support.

It was natural however, nay inevitable, to give credit to the spontaneous communications of my friends above alluded to. And the accuracy of these did not appear to me to be overturned by the assertions made by Mr. Montagu's relations and friends in the colony, that up to a certain period which they named, Lord Stanley's judgement of the case before him was in my favour.

Nevertheless, notes of approaching triumph were sounded louder and louder by Mr. Montagu's adherents. Revelations were made of the confidence reposed in Mr. Montagu by the Secretary of State; his appointment to the Secretaryship of the Cape of Good Hope was announced, and was spoken of by his friends as a promotion most congenial to his feelings, but this was considered hyperbolical. His successor in Van Diemen's Land was also named (in due time the Gazette notices in the London papers confirmed these appointments); and whilst all these matters were subjects of household discussion in every family in the colony, I remained unhonoured by any communication upon them from the Secretary of State.

The appointment to the Cape of Mr. Montagu, whom I had recommended for official employment in terms which could leave no doubt of my sincerity, did not in itself either surprise or displease me, but it did appear to me that the natural and proper order of things was somewhat reversed, when I had to learn from the private statements of an adverse clique and from the public prints, circumstances which in the highest degree concerned myself and my government.

Documentary evidence exists in my possession that Lord Stanley's despatch, which is at the head of this narrative, was known to be in the colony before I received it myself by the 'Duchess of Northumberland' in January 1843, and I have besides the testimony of a resident at Port Phillip, to its having been publicly read at a dinner-table in that colony at a date prior to my receipt of it. At the same time it was made known in Van Diemen's Land, from the same private sources of information, that Mr. Montagu's salary as Colonial Secretary was to be paid to him up to his departure for the Cape, the funds of the colony being thus to be made chargeable with the salaries of two Colonial Secretaries, of one of whom it was pronounced by Lord Stanley, that it was "highly inexpedient" to restore him to office. When I heard of this alleged decision of Lord Stanley's as to the salary, I made no scruple of replying that I *did not believe one word of it*; but *four months after*, in April 1843, I received from Lord Stanley a command to call upon the Legislative Council to vote this penalty upon the colony for my misdeeds.

Lord Stanley's despatch was received by me on the 18th of January 1843; all reserve was now thrown aside, and Mr. Swanston, manager of the Derwent Bank, the agent of Mr. Montagu and a member of the Legislative Council, placed a copy of it for general inspection on his office-table.

The public read at the same time with myself, how Her Majesty's minister thought proper to treat the representative of

Her Majesty's authority in a distant but most important colony, over which he was at that moment presiding.

Undoubtedly the Secretary of State was the judge to pronounce upon my act in having suspended the Colonial Secretary, and as he disapproved of that act, he was bound to convey his sentiments to both Mr. Montagu and myself. But I trust I am not overstepping the bounds of decorum, when speaking of my late official chief, in saying that he was bound also to respect the office I held and the character I bore. It was not owing to any consideration on Lord Stanley's part, if my government were not made, after the publication of his despatch, an object of contempt; and his lordship's imputation of want of energy and decision fell harshly and somewhat strangely on a man who had spent above forty years in the service of the crown, in almost every trying situation in which one of his profession could be placed, without a stain upon his character or an imputation on his capacity, until he had the misfortune of falling under his lordship's censure, for an act which might seem to indicate the very reverse of the weakness attributed to him.

Nor was it to have been expected, that because the duty of protecting my wife from the injurious statements which I believed Mr. Montagu was prepared to make against her, had obliged me to introduce her name into a despatch, her name should therefore have been placed at the head of one of Lord Stanley's divisions of the subject before him in terms of most ambiguous meaning.

The ink was scarcely dry on his lordship's despatch before its import was mentioned by a relative of Mr. Montagu's in the hall of the Admiralty : it was sent to Mr. Montagu, who it will be recollected was then on the spot, four days after its date, unaccompanied by any injunction of privacy, but on the contrary bearing on it the stamp of being Mr. Montagu's own authorized property, to be used as he thought proper.

Previous to receiving it, Mr. Montagu had been circulating a " *memorandum*," as he calls it, of the most defamatory character against me and my wife, in order to account for his removal from office, a copy of which memorandum is deposited in the Colonial Office; but after the receipt of this despatch, he put aside, as he very reasonably might, his memorandum, deeming his object perhaps nearly as well secured, and in a more legitimate manner, by the circulation of his lordship's document.

Accordingly Mr. Montagu spared no pains to give the official document publicity; it was discussed at the naval and military clubs,—disseminated undoubtedly, as he tells Lord Stanley his memorandum had been, in " *the very same society which his lordship himself frequented,*" and of course forwarded as we have seen to Van Diemen's Land, to Port Phillip, to Sydney, where it was brought under Sir George Gipps's observation, and wherever else it was capable of exciting any interest.

The despatch, as I have said, arrived on the 18th of January. In the ' Courier ' of the 20th is the following announcement: " We anticipate next week to be enabled to lay the substance of it before our readers;" it was not until several months later however that it appeared verbatim in the columns of the ' Courier ' newspaper *. Its appearance in this paper was announced by the following paragraph:—

" One word to the ' Advertiser ' before we have done. We agree with him that ' the open circulation of the opinion of Lord Stanley ' will give a zest to Mr. Montagu's triumph, and to mark our sense of the unanimity on this one point between ourselves and our contemporary, we promise to publish the despatch containing the decision of Lord Stanley in this notable case, in the next edition of the ' Courier.' "—*Courier*, June 30, 1843.

When the next edition of the Courier appeared on the 7th of July, I read, for the first time, the following letter from Mr. Stephen to Mr. Montagu, which formed a preface to the despatch:—

" SIR,   " Downing Street, 17th September, 1842.

" I am directed by Lord Stanley to transmit to you for your information a copy of Despatch (No. 150, 13th September 1842), which his lordship has addressed to Lieut.-Governor Sir John Franklin, communicating to him his opinion in regard to the circumstances which led to your suspension from the office of Colonial Secretary at Van Diemen's Land.

" You will consider that despatch as conveying to you his lordship's decision in your case†.

" I have the honour to be, Sir,

" Your most obedient, humble servant,

" *John Montagu, Esq., &c.*"   " JAMES STEPHEN."

* Mr. Montagu acknowledges, as will be afterwards seen, that he sent a copy to Mr. Forster and another to Mr. Swanston. The ' Courier ' also informs us that it *had its own copy*. This is an additional fact, the accuracy of which must be settled by Mr. Montagu and Mr. Elliston.

† It appears from Mr. Montagu's own statement, in a letter to the Secretary of State, dated 16th of January 1844, that his lordship's decision was verbally communicated by himself to Mr. Montagu on the 29th of August

It thus appeared that the possession by Mr. Montagu of a despatch addressed to myself was not, as I had at first vainly imagined, the result of inadvertence on Lord Stanley's part, or an unauthorized act of partiality on the part of any friend of Mr. Montagu's in that office, and misused by him, but the deliberate act of Lord Stanley himself, executed by his express command.

Mr. Montagu's reply to Lord Stanley's despatch was not published in Van Diemen's Land. It was of a character too vituperative towards myself, and revealed too plainly the unworthy method of defence which he had adopted, to make it safe or prudent to do so ; but it was circulated in manuscript, and alluded to in the public prints*.

The despatch and these accompaniments were in fact the leading theme of every local newspaper, and they were in most of them the text-book of every species of vulgar insult. The complimentary gift of a copy of the despatch to Mr. Montagu, the making *me* the recipient of the unbounded eulogium lavished upon *him,* and *him* the depository of the unmitigated censures bestowed upon *me,* was a course at once so unique and so ingenious, that it took the colony by surprise. The least that could be said of it by Mr. Montagu's relations and friends was, that it was an *unparalleled* instance of favour.

On the receipt of the despatch I hastened to request of Lord Stanley that he would lose no time in appointing my successor, unless he was enabled to give me the assurance of possessing, what this despatch seemed to render so equivocal, the continued confidence of Her Majesty's Government. But long before this conditional resignation could reach England, my successor was on his voyage out, and he arrived, as will be afterwards seen, in the colony four days before I received the official notice of my recall.

If it be wondered at, that instead of this conditional resignation I did not instantly throw up the government, I have no hesita-

(1842), and that " he did not expect a more formal announcement of the issue of his case."

* In the Appendix C. will be found a letter addressed by a gentleman whose testimony is unimpeachable, to an officer of my government, in which the impression produced on the writer by this letter of Mr. Montagu's is given.

The same letter contains a disclosure of considerable importance when viewed in connexion with some of Mr. Montagu's assertions, but which it would be premature here to dwell upon.

E

tion in declaring that such an act would have been a weak and cowardly surrender of the interests and welfare of the colony to my personal feelings, at a crisis of peculiar difficulty, and at the distance of what may be figuratively called a twelvemonth from home. It was the very act most desired by an agitating and mischievous faction, and that which would have neutralized the good I expected to realize by the removal of Mr. Montagu. I had no reason to suppose that Lord Stanley's despatch was meant to lead me to such a precipitate measure, or to indicate that my place was already understood to be vacant; but on the contrary I had grounds for thinking, as I have already stated, that it was Lord Stanley's intention and desire to retain me in the government. If it were otherwise, why did Lord Stanley not send back Mr. Montagu to an office, from which he had been, according to his lordship's judgement, unjustly displaced? Why had he acknowledged that it was highly inexpedient to do so? The restoration of Mr. Montagu must either have been inexpedient on public grounds, in which case I must have succeeded in making good in some degree my arguments against it, or it was inexpedient because Lord Stanley did not desire my resignation, which he knew must instantly have followed Mr. Montagu's reinstatement. His lordship having abstained from this act, I had no excuse for precipitately abandoning my post, which I conscientiously felt, under the circumstances in which the colony was then placed, would have been a most unjustifiable dereliction of my duty. It would besides have been a crowning triumph to a factious and insolent party, of which I meant to deprive them.

But this is not all. Lord Stanley's despatch was a mystery to me; it was inconsistent with itself, and impaired every preconceived idea I had formed of his justice and his courtesy; nay, it did more. Had Mr. Montagu been allowed to dictate the despatch to any subordinate in the Colonial Office, it could scarcely have more tenderly and delicately identified itself with him. Even the small measure of blame which is attributed to Mr. Montagu by Lord Stanley, being precisely that measure which Mr. Montagu takes to himself in his apologetic letter to me of the 31st of January 1842*, and no more, could not be

* Lord Stanley, it will be seen by a reference to the Despatch No. 150, " cannot acquit Mr. Montagu of having used, in the case of Dr. Coverdale, some language which I might not unnaturally regard as a menace," and considers that he is not altogether to be exempted from the reproach of having

avoided, though even this grain of censure is subsequently absorbed in the glowing and sweeping exculpation which relieves the ex-Colonial Secretary from every censure affecting not only the integrity, but even the *propriety* of his conduct. But whatever might have been the misgivings to which this singular and partial advocacy of Mr. Montagu gave birth in my mind, I did not commit the great blunder of revealing them. There was nothing in my reply to Lord Stanley which could indicate other than a full persuasion on my part, that I read his lordship's deliberate sentiments in his lordship's own selected words, which I was bound to receive with deference, even whilst I remonstrated against their application. My desire was to write with moderation as well as with respect, and if some warmth of expression was anywhere elicited from me, it was only when, in reference to the equivocal mention of Lady Franklin's name, I denounced the infamous intrigues by which it had been outraged, explained my motives for having brought it forward, and called upon his lordship's sense of justice as a minister, and of honour as a man, to put me in possession of those statements by which Mr. Montagu had established to his lordship's satisfaction, if such were indeed the case, a charge which was false in all its bearings. I told Lord Stanley, in reference to the public exposure of his despatch at the Derwent Bank, that I felt persuaded he had not contemplated such an indignity being offered to an officer still encumbered with the cares and responsibilities of government (being then ignorant that the copy of which Mr. Montagu had obtained possession was given by the express act of Lord Stanley), for that he knew my position, as the administrator of the affairs of the Government, could command respect only so long as it received it from the source whence it was derived; and reminded him of what he must be well aware of, that it would have been less painful to my feelings to have been relieved from my charge than to be placed in so embarrassing a situation. I assured him, however, that the good sense and good feeling of the community had repudiated the proceeding of Mr. Montagu and his agents, and had been evidenced by many personal assurances of respect and attachment which I had received in consequence of it.

It was by no means, I will venture to say, Lord Stanley's in-

substituted a service confined to the exact limits of positive duty, for that of a "cordial co-operation."

tention that I should precipitately throw up my government, nor did he anticipate any such occurrence. His lordship's policy, it would appear, was not only to retain me in the government until he had made all the new arrangements which followed his communication with Mr. Montagu in Downing-street, but to withhold from me the knowledge that any such changes were in contemplation. When the new Colonial Secretary left England, at the beginning I believe of December 1842, my recall was decided upon,—nay, was a matter, as I have since understood, of notoriety in England, though the name of the individual fixed upon as my successor had not publicly transpired; yet Mr. Bicheno was the bearer to me of no communication, either official or confidential, of the impending change. The letter by which Lord Stanley introduced him to me contained no intimation, that so soon as he and the Assistant Colonial Secretary who accompanied him had become initiated into their new duties, they would be followed by the new Governor, whose arrival was apparently delayed merely for the purpose of avoiding the embarrassment which might have attended the simultaneous arrival of so many new officers.

Mr. Bicheno brought me some important despatches from Lord Stanley respecting the changes which his lordship was about to introduce in prison discipline, and in those despatches I am addressed as the person who was at once to commence initiatory steps for this purpose; and my zealous solicitude was bespoken, or rather (apparently) confided in, for the due execution of the duties thus devolving upon me.

Nevertheless, these despatches, however calculated to mislead me as to the point in question, were, as well as others which I received at the period of Mr. Bicheno's arrival, in April 1843, of such a nature, that I could no longer doubt that the influence obtained by Mr. Montagu with Lord Stanley pervaded the dictation of the whole.

Mr. Montagu's arrival in England had been simultaneous with the urgent need then felt in Downing-street for the advice and information of some practical and intelligent man acquainted with the colony, in order to frame those instructions for the management of the convicts, which since the abolition of assignment I had been led, as I have before stated, to expect, and was anxiously awaiting from home. Mr. Montagu recommended himself, and was recommended to Lord Stanley as the very man to suit his lordship's purpose. So soon as Lord Stanley had decided upon the condemnation of my suspension of Mr. Montagu, and had bestowed upon him eulogiums, which, but for this propitious event, might never have been elicited, he could have had no scruple in availing himself of Mr. Montagu's services, and of admitting him to his utmost confidence. There could have been no objection, after Lord Stanley had with so little ceremony entirely set aside all my statements and preferred those of Mr. Montagu, that he should, in the despatches I now received on convict discipline, neglect altogether to notice that I had myself announced to him a plan for the management of the convicts, which must have been at that moment in operation in the colony, and the report of which must have been on its way home. Lord Stanley either wholly forgot that he had received such a despatch from me, or thought it not worth his while to wait for the Governor's opinions when he had the ex-Colonial Secretary by his side; whether my plans should be found to have anticipated his own, or to clash with them, was of little importance.

Accordingly Lord Stanley quotes to me the " very high authority of the late Colonial Secretary " for statements of a very startling nature, and never seems for a moment to suspect either that the late Colonial Secretary's data might be incorrect, or that his authority might, without prejudice to the case, have been veiled from my observation. Had I been aware that Mr. Montagu would have been so quickly called to his lordship's councils, I might have felt it my duty to have pointed out that my testimony to his fitness for office was not intended to apply to his being the adviser of Lord Stanley in all matters relating to Van Diemen's Land, and that upon convict matters, recent experience had proved to me the unsoundness of some of his views, and that his opinions on such a subject were liable to be biased by his family interests.

Though Mr. Montagu may have abundant proof to show that I at one time entertained different sentiments as to his judgement, he must also show, in order to convict me of inconsistency, that I have had no reason to change them.

I am not about to enter here into any elucidation of these remarks, or into an investigation of the new system sent out for me to initiate. In some of its features it resembled that which I had already brought into operation in the colony on my own responsibility, particularly as respected the distribution of the convicts after they had served their time in the labour-gangs into private service on wages; but under the present administration of the system, it appears to be freed from many of those restraints and checks by which I had endeavoured in this and subsequent stages of the prisoner's sentence to guard the interests and safety of the colonists, and to promote, as I conceived, the good conduct and moral benefit of the prisoners themselves. Experience will probably prove that the period of an excessive and uncontrolled increase of the convict population is not that in which a greater degree of license can be prudently accorded.

The only specific feature of the new system, as conveyed to me in Lord Stanley's despatch, which I shall here notice, is the appointment which his lordship announced to me of a new officer, to be called the Comptroller-General of Convicts, who was to unite in his own person the powers, if not the labours, of various subdivisions of the convict department, and was to communicate directly with the Governor, without the intervention of the Colonial Secretary; thus diminishing the labours and the influence of the latter officer, and transferring them to the new official, who would become in fact a second Colonial Secretary.

The Comptroller-General of Convicts Lord Stanley informed me was to be sent out from England, but this fact was considered doubtful by the Chief Police Magistrate of the colony, Mr. Forster, who had private reasons for believing that himself would be the person appointed, and some of the colonial papers of the day boldly promulgated his appointment. Whatever reasons I might have for regarding as authentic any anticipations entertained by Mr. Forster in general respecting his interests at the Colonial Office, I could not give any weight to such conjectures in the present instance, since not only was Lord Stanley's despatch before me, informing me that the Comptroller-General would be sent out from England, but also I considered, that in coming to this decision his lordship had been guided by the most judicious and sound policy. It was particularly desirable, that on the arrival of a new Governor so great an increase of political importance should not be bestowed on an individual already in long possession of official influence in another department intimately connected with that of the convicts, and in which he had had an army of subordinates at command. Such a concentration of personal influence and official powers might have a tendency to create a species of *imperium in imperio*, which would be neither convenient nor safe.

I have alluded to the general tenor of my communications in the month of April 1842, when the new Colonial Secretary arrived, as indicating the all-pervading influence of Mr. Montagu over his lordship's deliberations in the government of that colony.

It will be recollected that four months back there arrived in Van Diemen's Land private information addressed to Mr. Montagu's friends, that his salary was to be paid to him from colonial funds up to the date of his appointment to the Cape. Simultaneously with the arrival of the new Colonial Secretary came the order to me from Lord Stanley to call upon the Legislative Council for their approbation of this item in the estimates.

The execution of this order became the duty of my successor. I did not see it in the estimates which were brought by him before the Legislative Council previous to my departure from the Australian colonies, nor have I observed any notice of it whatever in the debates of Council.

Another despatch in the bag of the " John Renwick," in April 1843, demands a few words of notice ; it related to the Macquarie Harbour expedition mentioned in p. 40. I must premise, that this despatch, like every other which had a tendency to weaken my legitimate authority and impair the energies of my government, was announced by Mr. Forster's friends in the colony, and in the public prints, before it was transmitted to me. It began to be understood in the colony that the Governor's office was by no means the most authentic source of Downing-street information, and certainly it was not in possession of the earliest.

The despatch to which I am now alluding was founded on an insolent article in the ' Van Diemen's Land Chronicle' of the 3rd of May 1842, which attributes to me the granting indulgences, or remission of punishment, to certain prisoners who accompanied me in the expedition to Macquarie Harbour, in reward of their having acted as palanquin-bearers to Lady Franklin during a portion of that journey. I speak from memory, not having a copy of the newspaper in question by me. Lord Stanley, referring to the Gazette notice of the indulgence, and of course giving no " credit to the unworthy motives attributed to me," yet requests me to account for the unusual course which appears to have been taken on the occasion, and begs to know whether there was any truth in the assertion that they were thrice-convicted felons who had been thus pardoned by me.

It would be superfluous and tedious to enter here into the details, which, in obedience to Lord Stanley's command, I had the honour to submit to him in explanation of the corrupt conduct imputed to me; and this is the less necessary, since his lordship has condescended to assure me since my return to England, though not until I had made application on the subject, that he was satisfied with my explanation. The palanquin and its alleged occupant and its bearers formed however no part of my elaborate story.

But however grotesque may be the aspect of this incident, it was impossible for me not seriously to feel and to deplore the injury done to good government, by thus arraigning at the bar of judgement the governor of a colony, the representative of the Queen's authority there, on the absurd and abusive representations of a colonial newspaper; that colony also the farthest removed from the protection of Her Majesty's Government, the receptacle of her most refractory and lawless subjects; that newspaper the identical publication which I had already brought before Lord Stanley's notice as the most personally malignant and libellous of the local press, at the time when its especial object seemed to be the advocacy of Mr. Montagu's interests and purposes.

I ventured to assure his lordship in my reply to his despatch, that there was no respectable individual in the colony who did not already feel the injury done to his interests both at home and abroad by the licentious press of the colony, and who would not deplore that new aspect of importance which had now been given to it, by its being thus made the foundation of a despatch such as I had just received from him. I informed Lord Stanley that the subject of that despatch was already in the possession of Mr. Montagu's friends in the colony *before* it was transmitted to me, that the public were in possession of the fact through their means, but that of course they possessed it unaccompanied by the explanations I offered to his lordship, and which it was out of my power to lay before the public. In conclusion, I expressed my satisfaction at the assurance his lordship had given me, that he gave no credit to the unworthy motives attributed to me ; but I entreated him to do me the justice to believe that no suspicion would naturally enter my mind, that any but the highest motives could ever be attributed to me by Her Majesty's Government, for any exercise of the lawful authority vested in me.

In order to give Lord Stanley some idea of the use made of this occurrence, I transmitted to him a colonial newspaper (' Murray's Review '*), and called his attention to another statement made in the same newspaper, which seemed well calculated to arrest his lordship's attention. This was no other than the announcement of the author's intention to publish the correspondence which had passed between his lordship and Mr. Montagu on his late suspension. Whence were these interesting documents derived ? The answer is attached to a story which forms the most remarkable feature in my narrative.

When Mr. Bicheno, the new Colonial Secretary, arrived in Van Diemen's Land in April 1843, he brought with him under cover, a bound folio book of 312 manuscript pages. It was the document alluded to in page 5, at the commencement of this narrative, as forming a key to, and commentary upon, Lord

---

* " We rejoice to find that the newspaper press of this colony has such weight with the authorities at home as to produce despatches from the Secretary of State to the Lieutenant-Governor, calling upon that functionary for explanations upon points which the newspaper press had brought under public consideration. It will be remembered, that the late ' Van Diemen's Land Chronicle ' commented with much severity upon the fact, that the Lieutenant-Governor had *paid* the prisoners of the crown, employed by his excellency upon the late ' *book-making* ' expedition to Macquarie Harbour, as *palanquin*-bearers to Lady Franklin or some other of the *suite* of his excellency, by granting to them pardons ; a measure in itself extremely objectionable, and wholly uncontemplated by the Home Government, to be bestowed in remuneration for any services rendered for the personal accommodation of any governor. In consequence of the statement of our late contemporary, the Lieutenant-Governor has received a despatch from the Secretary of State, calling upon him to make known whether that statement is true, and if it is, to furnish the home authorities with a detail of the claims which the palanquin-bearers had to such indulgences. Sir John Franklin is therefore now compelled, and solely, the Secretary of State avows, in consequence of the representations of the newspaper press (the ' Van Diemen's Land Chronicle '), to render explanations which he will not only find difficult, *but which being so compelled to render*, must be productive of mortification to him, if he possesses the shadow of feeling, of the deepest mortification."—*Murray's Review.*

Stanley's despatch on Mr. Montagu's defence in Downing-street, both written and verbal; and under the latter head, a record of those defamatory statements I have alluded to.

The book was entrusted to Mr. Bicheno by Mr. Montagu, who did not explain to him its contents, with a request that it might be delivered to Mr. Forster. This officer, after reading, as he has stated, only a part of it, transmitted it according to Mr. Montagu's farther directions to Mr. Swanston, who extensively circulated it in the community. It was perused by the two Judges, by the leading counsel and solicitors of Hobart Town, by several Members of Council, by clergymen, by settlers in the interior, by some who had only to go to the Derwent Bank and request a sight of it, by others to whom, when it became convenient to deny its contents, it was offered, in order to enable them to swear to a deception of which they were not the dupes*.

The terms on which its perusal was granted were easy and safe. The readers were forbidden to copy it, but they might speak freely of its contents†. It was evident that the publication was complete, and that it was a publication in the worst and most injurious form.

---

* It seems scarcely credible that Mr. Swanston, bound by his oath as a Member of the Legislative Council to uphold the honour of his Sovereign, should have transmitted a book, the leading object of which was to traduce the representative of that sovereign, to a colonial newspaper, with the editor of which, communication or co-operation had until now been considered immeasurably detrimental; and with whom, if I have been rightly informed, the alleged intimacy of a public officer in the time of my predecessor had been brought forward as one of the grounds of his dismissal.

† The following extract from one of the local newspapers attaches more caution than was really observed to the conditions imposed upon the readers, but it characterizes accurately the underhand mode of its dissemination :— " The book was sent to some in confidence ; they were to read the book, not lend it, nor make known its contents, but they might give the results of their knowledge. They had an *ex-parte* statement, a collection of documents, notes of conversations, and statements which were to be received as facts : from the perusal of those they were to form a judgement, and to publish that judgement. But the documents, the notes of conversation, and the statements themselves, were to be carefully concealed : there was to be no opportunity given of combating or disproving them ; they were not to be even mentioned, lest they might be rebutted, but a conclusion was to be drawn from them and given to the public; and this, though some of them were false, and many distorted, though important facts relative to some were concealed, and others misstated. Verily we have heard of fair play in our time, and if this is honesty, we should wish to have a definition of treachery. What the opinions were notwithstanding, we may judge by the facts, that one confidant declared to Captain Swanston, that the book was unfit to meet the public eye, and that another flung it from him with disgust at its treachery, its meanness, and the calumnious nature of its contents."—*Hobart Town Advertiser*, June 26, 1843.

I should do injustice both to many of those who read, and to all of those who refrained from reading Mr. Montagu's book, did I not acknowledge both the high and honourable feeling which prevented the latter from indulging their curiosity, and the very natural and reasonable excuse of many of those who on the other hand yielded to the temptation. Who that had read Lord Stanley's despatch No. 150, and there were few in the colony who had not read it, but must desire to learn how Mr. Montagu had conducted a successful defence "which was not allowed to face its opponent," and to be made acquainted with the unexpected illumination which Mr. Montagu's revelations had now thrown upon it?

Mr. Montagu revealed to the public in Van Diemen's Land that his line of defence with Lord Stanley had been this,—he was the victim of Lady Franklin's hatred, and she alone was the cause of his suspension. To establish this point was the one leading object of Mr. Montagu's policy; for if established, Mr. Montagu conceived that all my official arguments and statements against him would fall to the ground, and appear only as the delusive representations by which I sought to disguise my own weakness; every effort therefore was concentrated upon this point. It was necessary in the first place to prove me a fool; accordingly I am represented as a perfect "imbecile," of whom it had been absolutely necessary that he (Mr. Montagu) should have the guidance, a fact sufficiently accounting for and excusing his undue assumption of power. It was necessary to vilify the character of Lady Franklin, and impute to her sufficient motives for her determination to get rid of him. She is represented as an "intriguing," "clever," "dangerous," "bad woman," and her hatred to Mr. Montagu as caused by his refusing to "pander" to her desire of travelling about the colony at the public expense*. It was most desirable that the act should be represented as her's alone, and that neither myself nor others should be accused of any participation in it, since that would have raised up defenders of the measure in the accused persons, or have helped to prove

* This charge, involving the very serious one of my misapplication of the colonial funds, was treated by me in my despatch to the Secretary of State with some detail. It is sufficient here to state that I informed his lordship that on no single occasion that I could bring to my recollection had the funds of the colony been called upon for Lady Franklin's purposes, and consequently that on no occasion whatever had Lady Franklin or myself been aware that Mr. Montagu refused to pander to such purposes.

that it was a right measure, and thus have weakened the pressure upon a helpless individual, and upon me, over whom it was to be shown that her influence was supreme. Accordingly Lady Franklin's name is the only one Lord Stanley is permitted to hear. Not one word is said by Mr. Montagu of that "*fierce phalanx of his enemies*" (to use his own expression) which surrounded me, and from which he expressed his belief in the hour of danger "that Lady Franklin alone could *save* me*;" not an allusion to my faithful and fearless private secretary, who, it may be recollected, had come prominently forward on his own personal responsibility, to obtain from Mr. Montagu a disavowal of the imputation attached to him in connexion with the abusive ' Van Diemen's Land Chronicle †.'

Mr. Henslowe's correspondence with Mr. Montagu respecting this newspaper was before Lord Stanley. It served probably only as another proof of Lady Franklin's enmity, since Mr. Montagu had not scrupled to state his belief at the time, not only that Lady Franklin was privy to, but that she dictated that correspondence.

It would take up too much time to enter into any detail of the various imputations made against my wife and myself in Mr. Montagu's record of his conversations with Lord Stanley, for it was in Lord Stanley's presence and into his ear and that of Mr. Hope, Under Secretary of State, that these defamatory statements had been poured. Some of them appear in the Appendix, in the racy account given by one of the readers of the ' Book,' as Mr. Montagu's manuscript volume was technically called in the colony, of the contents of that compilation; and those who have more curiosity on the subject may find them in

* This observation was made by Mr. Montagu to a mutual and intimate friend a few days before his suspension, with the intention, as it was understood, of its being repeated.

† This act on Mr. Henslowe's part had excited the resentment of Mr. Montagu, the more so as it was an unexpected return for the courtesies and blandishments which, after the misunderstanding on the Coverdale case, he had lavished on my private secretary for the first time since their intercourse had existed. The moment thus chosen appeared to Mr. Henslowe to be singularly ill-adapted for these flattering attentions, since it would have been an embarrassing and an unbecoming position for my private secretary, who was an inmate of my family, to commence a hitherto unsolicited friendship with Mr. Montagu, at a moment when the latter had withdrawn from all cordial co-operation with me, and when the intimacy between our respective families was at an end. But Mr. Montagu had previously instructed Mr. Henslowe to expect "squalls" from Downing-street, and to "look out for himself."— See p. 27.

the series of Van Diemen's Land Chronicles of an earlier period, which shadowed forth the coming book of Mr. Montagu with remarkable precision. It is sufficient here to state, that Mr. Montagu's catalogue of Lady Franklin's delinquencies embraces a most comprehensive range of subjects, from the establishment of a newspaper of her own*, to which she contributed articles

---

* About the time of Mr. Montagu's suspension, the 'Advertiser,' a paper not hitherto distinguished for any very steady support of government, passed into new hands, and opposed a firm and creditable opposition to the agitation movement and the abusive productions of the adverse party. Mr. Montagu's charge against Lady Franklin of her being connected with this newspaper is an illustration of that armour of recrimination in which he generally found it convenient to invest himself. The charge appears also in a portion of the written defence of Mr. Montagu, as given by him to Lord Stanley and published in the 'Courier' newspaper. On this account, though otherwise almost too ludicrous for refutation, I imposed upon myself the task of informing Lord Stanley that his assertion or rather insinuation (for Mr. Montagu had carefully thrown from himself the responsibility of it by stating, that it was the current report in Van Diemen's Land) was utterly untrue in every possible sense, either as applied to the newspaper in question or to any other, accompanying this denial by a letter to the same effect, addressed to my private secretary from the respectable proprietor and editor of the 'Advertiser,' who makes the additional remark in the character of an occasional visitor at Government House, that Lady Franklin had never conversed with him on any political subject whatever.

This is not an unfit place to remark, that when the 'Van Diemen's Land Chronicle' commenced its opposition to the Governor, and marked the moment of doing so, by attacking with every species of insult the Governor's wife, there appeared in its columns an impertinent paragraph upon the inroad made upon colonial funds for her convenience or pleasure by the hire of the 'Breeze' schooner. A very temperate article in reply appeared in the 'Courier' to the effect, that of all scandal the Lieutenant-Governor should at least have been safe from this. The author of this article, an understood contributor to the 'Courier,' must have been well-known to the Messrs. Macdowell, yet it suited their purpose to inform the public, as if on authority which could not be disputed, that the article was from Lady Franklin's pen, and that it was no longer made a secret of; and when this assertion was denied by the 'Courier,' the public were again informed by Mr. Macdowell, that he could not take the ghost's word for it, for that in addition to its forming the general topic of conversation before he alluded to it in his paper, the article itself bore *internal evidence* of its manufacture, and that the testimony of his own senses must be abandoned, before he could abandon his conviction as to its origin. And here the matter rested for nearly two years, when the publication in Mr. Montagu's book of his insidious and safe imputation against Lady Franklin, respecting the 'Advertiser,' revived the remembrance of it, and induced my private secretary to request of Mr. Bradbury, Secretary to the Board of Education, whom he knew to be the author, his written avowal of it, in order that unanswerable evidence might in this one tangible instance be afforded of the falsehood and misrepresentation to which Lady Franklin had been exposed. Mr. Bradbury, thus called upon, unhesitatingly avowed himself the author of the article, adding that it was written " without the slightest suggestion from any person whatever." The correspondence between Mr. Henslowe and Mr. Bradbury appeared in the 'Advertiser,' and though Mr. Bradbury could show that he had made no *gratuitous* avowal of the truth,—that in fact he had done

from her pen, to the countermanding of Mr. Montagu's supply of plums and cabbages from the Government-gardens *.

The college also, the new government-house, the despatches, of which she is represented as the sole writer, all find a place in the indictment, and in case any or all of the charges should fail, her general interference with the government comes in to supply the deficiency.

With regard to myself, the chief charge in addition to my general imbecility, is the falsehood by which I had supported the St. George's Church case, and which is said to have done me more injury with Lord Stanley than anything else in my despatches, particularly as being an after-charge on my part; and secondly, the treachery I had shown in writing home in a despatch relating to Mr. Montagu's suspension, statements extremely injurious to Dr. Turnbull and Mr. Forster, which I concealed from them, and which are contrasted with statements of an opposite character respecting these gentlemen addressed by me to Mr. Montagu himself. The former charge is treated in Appendix D. Upon the latter, which is also alluded to in the first part of Mr. Young's letter, I shall say a few more words, as it gives a remarkable illustration of the evils against which I had to contend in my government at this period, and of the unworthy means employed to alienate from me the attachment and fidelity

that only which no gentleman or man of honour could help doing, this unexpected exposure was not forgiven.

* The charge of stopping Mr. Montagu's supply of fruit and vegetables is supported in the 'Book' by a letter from Mr. Herbertson, Superintendent of the Government-garden, in which he is made to state that he had stopped them by Lady Franklin's order (at a period shortly preceding Mr. Montagu's suspension). Knowing that Lady Franklin had never given any such order, or caused it to be given, I desired that Mr. Herbertson might be examined before the police magistrate of Hobart Town, when he made his declaration that he had never written any such letter as the one given in the book; that the initial letter of his christian name, said to be affixed to the letter in the book, was not his own, and moreover that he never received any such order from Lady Franklin as that contained in the letter, either written or verbal.

The following is the manner in which the 'Van Diemen's Land Chronicle' prepared me a year or two before to anticipate Mr. Montagu's story. I quote one only of many passages to the same effect, dispersed through the pages of that paper :—

" Lady Franklin however can inflict all these injuries by directly interfering in the affairs of government, and yet pass without observation, nay with a certain degree of applause before the world. She proceeds to Government-garden and *suspends* a supply of vegetables to Captain Montagu's house before he is deprived of his office. This, in itself, is a very *little* act, but yet it betrays much, and will be quoted in the London circles with immoderate laughter."— *Van Diemen's Land Chronicle*, February 11th, 1842.

of one of my most worthy officers. The dissimulation and double-dealing here attributed to me were calculated to injure me greatly in the colony amongst all who found it difficult to believe that so bold an assertion could be made without any foundation in fact. With Lord Stanley, if his lordship condescended to read or inquire into the contents of his own despatches or into those of his predecessors, it could do me no injury, as he would find that I had written home no such statement as the one imputed to me; that with regard to Mr. Forster, I had scrupulously forborne to implicate him in the detail of circumstances which led to Mr. Montagu's suspension; and as respects Dr. Turnbull, had never omitted an opportunity of speaking of him in terms of the highest commendation and friendship.

Dr. Turnbull had no reason to doubt this fact; but what could he do, when informed by Mr. Forster several months before the arrival of the same story in Mr. Montagu's book, that I had written secretly against him to the Colonial Office, and that Mr. Montagu, then in England with access to that office, was his authority? What could Dr. Turnbull do, when his informant, Mr. Forster, laid upon him an injunction of secrecy, which made it impossible for him to reveal this painful communication to me, and relieve his mind of the suspicions insinuated? The painful impression thus produced upon Dr. Turnbull's mind was such, that he hesitated before he accepted a private invitation to spend the Christmas with me and my family in the country; and though the conflict of his feelings was at last ended, it was by the exercise of his own faith in my honour, and not by any elucidation of facts. From this satisfaction, his unguarded pledge of secrecy had precluded him; and when it was observed that our friendly relations continued unbroken, it was made a subject of reproach to him, as arguing a degree of insensibility to right and wrong which could not fail to injure his prospects " *under a new Governor**." When Mr. Montagu sent out this tale of my falsehood and treachery, in the first instance in a letter to Mr. Forster, he must either have known it to be a fiction, or he was grossly misinformed; but between that period and the transmission, some months later, by Mr. Bicheno of the 'book,' in which a second edition of the story appears, he must have convinced himself of his error, if it were one, and was bound in his book not to have repeated, but to have contradicted it. The bane how-

---

* Mr. Swanston's words.

ever was forwarded to the colony without the antidote. [See the letter in the Appendix D. of Mr. Young, who thought it necessary to warn Dr. Turnbull against me as a person not to be trusted.] I shall say no more on this subject except to state, that on becoming acquainted with these charges against my good faith, I submitted unreservedly to Dr. Turnbull, to whom it was due, and to Mr. Forster, to whom it was not due, all the despatches I had sent home respecting Mr. Montagu's suspension.

From the above notices of the contents of Mr. Montagu's book, it is not to be wondered at that the general testimony of its readers pronounced it to be " pernicious," " highly injurious," " mean," " underhanded," " pitifully malicious," " highly improper," " a moral assassination," " calculated to lessen the authority and respect due to the representative of the sovereign," and indicating in Captain Swanston, from whom the readers derived the ' book,' a " direct intention to bring His Excellency's government into contempt*."

It was evidently a libel of the most flagrant and injurious character, since its tendency and object were not only to defame my personal character and that of my wife, but to embarrass and impede my government and to produce disorder and agitation in the community. It is my firm belief, that had I succeeded in getting the book into my own hands, and had brought it before the Supreme Court of Van Diemen's Land, laying my damages at what amount I pleased, there is not a jury which could have been impanelled in the colony, which would not have returned me a verdict to the full amount. A recent libel case in Van Diemen's Land, which grew out of this ' book ' transaction, and which was not tried until after my departure from the colony, fully justifies my assertion†.

---

* Mr. Forster's determination after a partial perusal, "*not to read the book during the period of His Excellency's remaining in this colony*," proves that it must have been known to him to contain matter in reference to me unfit for him to possess.

† I allude to the cause of Gregson *v.* Dobson. Mr. Gregson is one of the oldest colonists of Van Diemen's Land, a man of education and talent, and of independent and honourable sentiments. After the removal of Mr. Montagu, between whom and himself there was the most irreconcileable opposition of interests and feelings, I appointed him, pending Her Majesty's pleasure, to a seat in the Legislative Council. The appointment was displeasing to the friends of Mr. Montagu, and I received from Mr. Dobson, a solicitor of Hobart Town, and an intimate friend and connexion of Mr. Swanston's, a remonstrance upon the subject, denouncing Mr. Gregson in the most libellous terms in connexion with some intricate transactions in which he was stated to have been

I was absent at Launceston when Mr. Montagu's 'book' came into circulation at Hobart Town. On my return thither the public mind was in a state of great excitement. The revelations of the 'book' had dropped, like sparks of fire upon the sun-dried herbage, into the most combustible of populations,

engaged. Knowing that the exposure of this document would set the community in a blaze, and having no doubt of Mr. Gregson's integrity, I submitted the paper to the acting Attorney-General, who advised me to decline entering into the investigation, and the decision to which I came upon this official "opinion" was communicated to the parties concerned. Their next step was to send me a copy of a letter addressed to the Secretary of State, which I was informed was to be transmitted to him by a ship then on the point of sailing for Bombay. I replied that my despatches would go by another ship, and my transmission of any documents upon the subject in question would depend upon my receiving them *in time* (for the observations I might be disposed to make upon them). No documents were ever sent to me, but the letter transmitted by India to the Secretary of State arrived in Downing-street while Mr. Montagu was in England. It would appear that in this *ex-parte* statement, Mr. Gregson was presumed to be guilty, for the confirmation of my appointment of him to the Legislative Council was withheld during my administration. The Derwent Bank party and its organs of the press exulted over the symptom, and prophesied his ignominious dismissal. To my successor was assigned the task of investigating the charges which the Secretary of State had received by the unofficial channel described. Sir Eardley Wilmot would appear to have felt embarrassed by the commission, and advised Mr. Gregson, who had before this time been made aware by me of the charges sent home against him, to bring his case into the Supreme Court; he did so,—laid his damages at £5000, (for the charges against him involved falsehood, fraud and perjury,) pleaded his own cause, and obtained a verdict from the jury to the full amount of the damages laid. The jury was a common one, the defendant having refused a special jury, though Mr. Gregson offered to let him strike the whole. [This is a circumstance, which, as the introduction of civil juries in Van Diemen's Land was an act of my administration, I regard with satisfaction, as an instance of its judicious working.] The trial lasted from the 19th to the 26th of March 1844. An effort was made by the defeated party, on account of the enormous damages, to procure a second trial, but it totally failed, the judges declaring that £5000, £10,000, or even £20,000 would not be sufficient compensation for so malicious a libel.

During the trial, repeated allusion was made to the scandalous libels of Mr. Montagu's book, for it was owing to that publication that Mr. Gregson first became acquainted with the infamy which it had been sought to cast upon his own character. Mr. Gregson had been one of the first persons to draw my attention to the "moral assassination," as he termed it, of Mr. Montagu's work; this he did in an official letter to my private secretary, and having thus boldly denounced and characterized the act, he desired that a copy of his letter might be sent to Mr. Swanston, the chief agent in the dissemination of the defamatory production. Mr. Swanston replied by forwarding to me a letter for transmission to Lord Stanley, referring to the tainted character of Mr. Gregson as it was deposited in the records of Lord Stanley's office; this letter, as well as the former one of Mr. Dobson's, hitherto withheld from him, I communicated to Mr. Gregson, and hence all that followed.

In the course of the trial in the Supreme Court, an effort was made by Mr. Macdowell, counsel for the defendant, to convict me of having suppressed a letter forwarded by Mr. Dobson for transmission to the Secretary of State. Mr. Macdowell supported this grave charge upon the evidence of my late pri-

F

and had spread with a celerity that baffled all restraint; there was an itching curiosity to know the full measure and quality of these revelations, and the appetite grew with the samples which were given to satisfy it.

Mr. Montagu's book was at the height of its publicity when a circumstance occurred which produced a startling effect upon the public mind, and no little consternation and surprise even amongst his nearest relatives and friends.

The public had read in its pages that it was by the vilification of a lady that Mr. Montagu boasted he had achieved his own exculpation to the entire satisfaction of the Secretary of State, and in particular, that he had left no means untried to prove that, from the beginning to the end, she was the author of his suspension.

The public now learned for the first time that it was his own appointed advocate that he had thus traduced, and that the influence which he had represented to Lord Stanley as all-powerful and malignant, had been used to save him, and had proved too weak for his purpose.

A rumour of this nature having gained ground in the community, was extremely unacceptable to Mr. Montagu's relations and friends. They had been kept in ignorance of the fact, and Mr. Swanston and Mr. Forster, in the presence of Dr. Turnbull, pronounced it to be without foundation.

Dr. Turnbull, considering himself bound by a promise to Mr. Montagu to keep his secret, was silent; but being called upon by me, and advised by the elders of his church (before whom he carried the case), to reveal the whole truth and protect Lady Franklin, he gave his testimony to the accuracy of the facts stated, and entered into details which proved the freshness of all the circumstances of this transaction in his memory. The effect produced by this disclosure was such, that even Mr. Montagu's best friends knew not how to defend him. Mr. Forster indeed caused Lady Franklin to be informed* by Dr. Turnbull, that he (Mr. Forster) had done her great injustice, having been

vate secretary Mr. Henslowe, now Police Magistrate of Campbeltown, whose evidence however being directly subversive, Mr. Macdowell was called upon to withdraw the charge in the same public manner in which it had been announced, which was done accordingly.

* Mr. Forster's personal intercourse with my family ended soon after that of Mr. Montagu.

ignorant up to that moment of Mr. Montagu's conduct in this affair, but Mr. Forster did not authorise Dr. Turnbull to make this acknowledgement generally known.

A reference to the local journals at this period will show that the slanders of Mr. Montagu's book, especially in respect to the new story just revealed respecting his application to Lady Franklin, but which had no place in that compilation, took possession of the public mind, to the exclusion of almost every other subject of interest. The newspapers in the interest of Mr. Montagu did what they could to pervert and mystify facts. On the other side his conduct was either held up to execration in no measured terms, or formed the subject of keen and bitter sarcasm.

It was time to check if possible this state of things. I had clearly a right to be put in possession of documents which were so detrimental to my own character and so destructive to the peace of the community; accordingly, on the 26th of May, I called on Mr. Swanston, as Lieutenant-Governor, and in that capacity, as President of the Legislative Council, of which he was a member, to deliver up to me Mr. Montagu's book. The book was at once withdrawn from circulation, but Mr. Swanston took ten days, during which period I renewed my application, before he was prepared to send me his reply, which was an " unqualified denial" of the nature and character attributed to the " documents referred to," and a refusal to give up the book, on the ground of its being a " private communication." I made a similar application to Mr. Forster with the same result. I have already shown how far such an assertion was available; and if I were to mention a few of the persons who had the reading of the book, it might be a matter of surprise that Mr. Swanston had not better consulted Mr. Montagu's reputation than by stating that he had sent it only to a very few of Mr. Montagu's " personal friends *." Mr. Young's letter (see Appendix D.)

---

* A colonial writer observes, " Mr. Montagu's friends draw largely on the simplicity of their admirers, when assuming that the book stands on the footing of a private communication. From a letter the intention of a writer may be incorrectly inferred : he may express himself in the warmth of unpremeditated composition : he may disclose to a friend what he would not confide to the world ; but when copies are bound up and forwarded in various directions, it *may happen* that they are unread, but then it may be safely concluded that the design has been frustrated.

" In Captain Forster we have an instance either of remarkable caution or unusual indifference. He did not read the book himself but handed it to his friend. But the world in general is more curious : and Captain Montagu did not miscalculate when he expected from the curiosity of the public greater suc-

will show how much claim that gentleman had, amongst the respectable readers of the ' book,' to be considered a personal friend of Mr. Montagu; but when Mr. Swanston penned this paragraph, he did not foresee that Mr. Young's letter would ever be written. It was clear, that if privacy had been intended by Mr. Montagu, which is not pretended, Mr. Swanston, his agent, must have violated it in every possible way.

The cause of Mr. Swanston's delay in answering my letter was afterwards revealed to me on testimony of unquestionable authority. The most offensive passages in Mr. Montagu's book had been removed, and Mr. Swanston was then able to give his " unqualified denial " to their existence.

That the original work was libellous and actionable, I consider confirmed by this act of precaution on Mr. Swanston's part.

In consequence of Mr. Swanston's and Mr. Forster's refusal

cess. In our apprehension the intention is not improved by a measured concealment—the prohibition of copying and extracting from the contents. It no doubt has prevented his Excellency from offering a direct refutation ; but it reflects no honour on his assailant.

" The contents of the book are differently described; but we may safely assume that it is calculated, not only to injure Sir John Franklin in his private capacity —not only to vex and annoy him—but to undermine the moral weight of his government * * * When the history of the book reaches the Colonial Office the result may be seen without a spirit of prophecy. * * *

" We are relieved from the necessity of arguing that the circulation of a book, injurious to any individual in a manner which shuts him out from reply and defence, is a violation of justice. Those who palliate the affair show their sentiments by their excuses. The book was under the charge of secrecy ; men of prudence and respectability alone were to read it ; extracts were forbidden; its circulation was to be cautious and limited : all which assumes that no man can appear in the face of day and assert that he would acknowledge the candour and honour of an adversary, who should bind up accusations and send them everywhere but to the house they defamed and the person whom they condemned. * * * It is not derived from the laws of chivalry, or the rules of polite society, or courts of justice, but from the common sense of reasonable beings, that if a charge is circulated to the disparagement of an individual by those who move in the same circle, he is entitled to hear it. * * * *

" Mr. Montagu is said to complain that Lady Franklin's influence is omnipotent. His own experience does not, however, support his allegation. It appears that, when dismissed from his office, he invoked her ladyship's mediation. It was employed, and it failed. Had he distrusted her sincerity, would he have sought her aid ? The *Review* is evidently embarrassed with the inconsistency between the charge and the proof; but by a device such as only occurs to practised ingenuity, he has attempted to remove the difficulty. Mr. Montagu did employ Lady Franklin ; that is admitted. He sent her on an errand of peace ; that is acknowledged : but she was authorized only to bear an offer of pardon to her rebellious husband ! After this, imagination must droop her wings, and conjecture can accomplish no more. But when she failed, ought Mr. Montagu, like a defeated suitor, to turn his back upon the bench and to charge his counsel with perfidy ?" * * *—*Launceston Examiner*, July 12, 1843.

to give up the 'book,' it became necessary for me to take in a tangible form the evidence of its contents from some of its readers.

A portion of this I transmitted to Lord Stanley, with remarks upon its nature and upon the obstacles which had attended its production. Of these documents, the only one I shall here adduce is the letter already mentioned of Mr. Young, addressed to my private secretary (see Appendix); and I do this with the less scruple, because, as will be seen, it is the testimony, I am far from saying of an enemy, but of one who had no desire at that time to be considered as a friend, and because the reasons which induced him to write it, viz, to expose the falsehoods of 'Murray's Review' in Mr. Montagu's case, are such as to preclude the supposition that publicity can be objectionable to him. I will only add, as to the value of this testimony, that Mr. Young is a solicitor of the first respectability in Hobart Town, and a man of unimpeachable integrity and great independence of character; in other respects, one who when he chooses to speak his mind speaks it freely, and, as my readers will judge, without any choice of courtly expressions.

It would be easy for me to bring forth proof upon proof, not only of the accuracy of all that I have stated respecting Mr. Montagu's book, but of the apprehensions of danger and injury to themselves which were felt by individuals when called upon to give testimony to facts which were adverse to the interests of the Derwent Bank*, and to those of an ascendant and vindictive

---

* "The Review asks, 'what object could Captain Swanston have in making so general an exhibition of the book?' Does he forget who and what Captain Swanston is, and on what his colonial influence depends? That he held a high station, not because he was Captain Swanston, or even because he was rich, but because he was the representative of 270,000*l.* of mortgages, which extended his influence into the houses of half the colony? That by the same means, and combined with him, he had the influence of the principal executive officer of the government? That these two, and they almost alone, were the representatives in the colony of the mass of wealth centred in the Derwent Bank, that the alliance of the Colonial Secretary was of the utmost importance in supporting his influence, and that by the act of the Governor he lost it? Any chance of recovering such influence was grasped at with avidity. To gain general credence for the report, that the power of the Governor was obliged to succumb to that of Captain Montagu, would at once restore this very influence, and we have seen the means he took to effect it. Had he been successful, he would at once have confirmed his own personal power and supported the Derwent Bank. Is any other cause wanted? Was it nothing to have the power to annoy, and, if possible, injure the Governor, to whose act, in removing his colleague, he owed his altered situation and diminished power? power diminished in one respect, but still great, and which, without much care, may

party. I shall be borne out in my assertion by the knowledge and experience of the community in Van Diemen's Land, when I assert that a general impression had long prevailed in that colony, and was justified by facts, that whoever offended that party, was sure, sooner or later, to suffer for it.

Nothing but the fear of designating individuals to their injury, and an unwillingness to name them even in the absence of such fear without their consent, prevents me from giving illustrations of this fact, which are more to the purpose than anything I have submitted to Lord Stanley.

The painful task remained to me, of communicating to Lord Stanley the unexpected revelation Mr. Montagu had made of his proceedings in Downing-street, and the wretched tissue of intrigues by which this disclosure had been made an instrument for undermining my government and destroying the peace and order of the community.

It would have been consolatory to me, if I could have deemed it superfluous to add any comments or explanations of my own, for the repudiation of Mr. Montagu's aspersions; but the events of the last few months, and those which were now disclosing themselves, convinced me that to trust to Lord Stanley's rejection of them, or his reprobation, would be on my part a blind presumption. It was evident that Mr. Montagu's defence, though on every point so clear and convincing as to leave to Lord Stanley only the choice of varied modes of expression by which to convey the self-same and " entire satisfaction " he had in it, was yet of a nature that it could not be revealed to me. This mystery was cleared up and accounted for by the " conversations." Mr. Montagu published what Lord Stanley desired to withhold; and the question was no longer, why did Lord Stanley *withhold* Mr. Montagu's statements, but why did he *accept* them?

Mr. Montagu has objected to any portions of his book being entitled " notes of conversations," but designates them as merely statements made verbally to Lord Stanley and Mr. Hope,

be the means of again establishing his former ascendency? It will be difficult for any future Colonial Secretary to resist the claim of Captain Swanston, backed by the opinions of men chained to his interests by the weight of 270,000*l.* of incumbrances, most of whom owe their very existence as landholders by his mere sufferance. * * * * * No one can deny the influence; it is as evident as noonday, and not the less that it places a considerable portion of the press completely at his feet."—*Hobart Town Advertiser*, June 20, 1843.

without his lordship's or his under secretary's answers. The
distinction is of little moment; the very argument itself goes
to prove that Mr. Montagu was unchecked in his imputations
on my character and efficiency, and in his statements regarding Lady Franklin. There does not appear to have been a
single word of remonstrance,—of disapprobation ; no voice to
defend the accused because the accused was absent, no remark upon the *gratuitous* nature of such vituperations, since
Mr. Montagu had been already exonerated from blame—praised
—promoted !

But Lord Stanley has not only left uncounteracted the appearance of his having so accepted Mr. Montagu's statements,
but by giving publicity to a despatch from which such a conclusion is necessarily inferred, has increased the injury to an in-
definite extent. I have no doubt that there was in Lord Stanley's mind an entire absence of any specific intention of this
kind; but his lordship has rigorously abstained from the condescension of telling me so.

It is evident that I was now forced, by the very nature and
necessity of the case, to bring Lady Franklin's name again before
him ; for I had to protect and defend her against charges made,
and revealed to have been made, in his lordship's office, and
which therefore could neither be regarded and put aside as idle
gossip, nor reserved for private refutation at some future period,
if an opportunity for such should be granted to me. I had no
other certain way of making known my contradiction of Mr.
Montagu's imputations, and my sense of their nature and object,
than by dealing with them directly and plainly ; and by proving
that the very effrontery of his policy, which was a dangerous
one, had ensured its success.

To the sweeping accusation of Lady Franklin's interference
with all the departments of government, and her unlimited influence over me (a state of things which Mr. Montagu, who
considered it necessary " to have the guidance of me," must
have found extremely inconvenient), I gave as serious and as
unqualified a denial as if the charge had been one which the
Secretary of State for the Colonies was perfectly able to appreciate, and fully justified to accept, in explanation of the ex-
Colonial Secretary's misconduct.

But Mr. Montagu's charge, whether derived exclusively from
his personal knowledge of Lady Franklin, or from the more

intimate acquaintance which Mr. Forster first cultivated with her during Mr. Montagu's absence, demands a moment's consideration.

It will be recollected, that on Mr. Montagu's departure for England in 1839, he professed the greatest possible regard for Lady Franklin, regretted that he had not known her more intimately at an earlier period, asked for her opinions, requested them even in writing for his own use in England, extolled her exertions to do good, and acknowledged himself under great personal obligations for kindnesses received. It is to be presumed therefore, that up to this time, her mischievous interference in public matters had not come under his cognizance or censure.

On Mr. Montagu's return to Van Diemen's Land, Lady Franklin was absent from the colony. It must therefore have been during the period of about four months only, previous to the Coverdale affair, that her evil influence became so apparent to Mr. Montagu; he then selected, amongst whatever instances in proof of it which he had in store, that instance undoubtedly which he thought not the *weakest,* but the *strongest.*

His delusion on this head furnishes a standard by which to judge of the truth and accuracy of his judgements in all similar cases; her universal agency is not brought forward until her particular agency is proved to be false.

But Mr. Montagu has a *letter* in his possession from Lady Franklin which he received in England, and in all probability he has among his stores of memoranda, many a note of her conversations, which, in the absence of more legitimate proofs, might serve his object at the Colonial Office, did he permit himself to make use of them.

One of the very few observations which I have heard attributed to Lord Stanley, in the conversations recorded between him and Mr. Montagu in Downing-street, had reference to this practice of Mr. Montagu's of making notes of private conversations to be laid by for use. The alleged observation of Lord Stanley was one natural to an honourable-minded man in his lordship's station; it expressed his disapprobation of such a practice. Though I cannot vouch for the accuracy of this circumstance, since I did not receive it on the same testimony as that which establishes the contents of the 'book,' yet I shall not permit myself to believe that one-sided and unverified testimonies of this nature, to give them no harsher name, are documents received at the Colonial Office in proof of any injurious accusations against the absent and the defenceless.

Of the letter alluded to I may have again occasion to speak; it is sufficient here to say, that it was written by Lady Franklin to Mr. Montagu in the confidence of friendship; with no fear of treachery before her eyes; with the vivid remembrance of his desire that she would give him her written opinions upon any subject which could benefit the colony while he was in England; with no notion that any political importance could be attached to any suggestion made in that letter, bearing as it did upon the face of it, and avowedly, that it had as yet received no sanction from me, and with the certainty that her words could have no other weight or efficacy with Mr. Montagu than that which he might himself think proper to give to them*.

Upon the friendly and confidential intercourse which Mr. Forster, while Acting Colonial Secretary in Mr. Montagu's absence, cultivated with Lady Franklin, I shall abstain from making any observations. It was sought for by him and frankly entered into by her, and has doubtless placed him in possession of her opinions on many points. The position thus created for himself by Mr. Forster was maintained by him until the period of Mr. Montagu's return from England.

But lest these explanations should be understood in a sense beyond my intention, I must permit myself one or two remarks.

If I wished to deny that Lady Franklin took a deep and most anxious interest in the welfare of the colony, which she knew to be the object of my own daily solicitude, there are many things that would tell a different story.

Mr. Montagu also may possibly be aware, that if at any time I have been in want of any help which Lady Franklin was capable of giving me, I have not hesitated to avail myself of it. There was a season indeed when some domestic aid was almost indispensable to me, owing to the want of a private secretary. This is a fact quite consistent with the formal denial, if it be necessary, of Lady Franklin's interference in the government, or of her being the general despatch-writer. No one knows better than Mr. Montagu how to make this distinction, and I

---

* It may not be unimportant to add, that though Lady Franklin has no note or memorandum of her letter to Mr. Montagu, yet that I retain a very clear and lively remembrance of the main and subordinate subjects of it, as reported by her to me within a very few hours after it was written.

would ask, where is the man who would scruple, on occasion, to avail himself of the capacity of his wife, when he knows the conscientious earnestness with which she enters into the feelings and responsibilities arising out of his public duties?

I have, perhaps unnecessarily, said as much to Lord Stanley. If, read by the light of Mr. Montagu's verbal statements, my words have conveyed to his lordship an impression entirely different from their intended meaning and from the facts of the case, and inconsistent therefore with the full denial given above, it must be, that being proof against the sneers of any man on this point, I did not sufficiently guard the candour of my admissions by an explanation of the stringent limits within which I expected them to be understood.

There were two subjects (as I have had the honour of informing Lord Stanley in illustration of some of Mr. Montagu's positions) in which Lady Franklin took an earnest and anxious interest; these were, education, and the reformation of the criminal, particularly of the female criminal. On the latter subject, Lady Franklin carried on a correspondence with Mrs. Fry, at the particular request of the latter lady, who submitted portions of it to Lord Stanley, which were retained in the Colonial Office.

It would appear that Lord Stanley did not consider this as improper interference in the Government, since he furnished a gentleman sent out to investigate the state of the convict boys' establishment in Van Diemen's Land, with a copy of portions of Lady Franklin's letter, and conveyed to her also by the same person a kind message respecting it.

Under the head of education, the other subject alluded to, I must say a few words on the College which I attempted to found in Van Diemen's Land, not only because it makes a formidable figure in Mr. Montagu's accusations against Lady Franklin in his book, but because it was a measure of my government to which I attached much importance.

I had not been long in Van Diemen's Land before I became sensible of the absence of any adequate education, beyond a few private schools, for the higher or wealthier classes of society, and especially of the want of some endowed institution analogous to the Etons and Rugbys of England, which might be capable of encouraging the students to pursue a course of liberal education beyond those mere years of childhood, which are all that are in general given to it in a money-making colony: something moreover which might tend to attach the resident to the soil, and make it really to him, what it professedly is in after-dinner speeches, his " adopted land."

Some efforts had been made in the time of my predecessor to establish a superior public seminary of education, but they appear to have had no result, owing, I believe, to the diversity of opinions which prevailed respecting its religious principles and arrangements. Sufficient encouragement however was stated to have been given to Sir George Arthur's views to enable me to hope that another effort in the same direction, and with higher aims, might be successful. In order to avoid at the outset any conflicting views, I deemed it advisable not to explain my own till I had taken the first step towards their accomplishment. Instead therefore of submitting my plans to public discussion, or even to a more limited scrutiny, I preferred communicating at once with my friend the late Dr. Arnold of Rugby, of whom also I requested the great favour of selecting a person fitted for the important charge contemplated, and of recommending such person to the Secretary of State for nomination. This was in the latter end of 1838. My letter, which contained, besides its immediate object, much necessary information on the state of society in Van Diemen's Land, and the prospects and resources of the colonists, I enclosed open to Lord Glenelg, with a request that if his lordship approved of my suggestions, he would forward it to Dr. Arnold. This was accordingly done by Lord Normanby, the successor of Lord Glenelg in office, with whom Dr. Arnold kindly undertook to negotiate the terms upon which he considered it essential that the " Principal " should be appointed. It was not until the beginning of 1840, however, during Mr. Montagu's absence in England, that I received from Lord Normanby his lordship's official approbation of my proposal, with all the correspondence between the Colonial Office and Dr. Arnold to which it had given rise.

In April 1840, Mr. J. P. Gell, M.A., of Trinity College, Cambridge *, selected by Dr. Arnold as being eminently qualified to be the superior of the College, and who had received Lord Normanby's nomination, came out to Van Diemen's Land, and

* Now the Rev. J. P. Gell.

in the following session of the Legislative Council, I read an elaborate minute on the foundation I wished to recommend to their adoption and endowment, and stated that I had already represented to the Secretary of State the importance of obtaining for it a royal charter*. The proposal was listened to with great interest and carried through the Council with only two dissentient voices. Money was voted for the erection of the College buildings, for the foundation of scholarships, and for the means of immediately commencing the Queen's School, an initiatory institution which was intended to prepare boys for the future College; and whilst this was going on in the Council, addresses came in from various districts of the island expressing the sense of the colonists upon the great benefit about to be conferred upon them, their opinions upon the religious principles on which it should be based, and their desire that the locality should be fixed within their respective district limits. The latter petitions were backed by promises of specified subscriptions to a large amount, in case of such localities being selected. In fact one part of the colony was bidding against another, which should have the College within its limits.

I fixed upon a site, which proved to be the same as that which Lady Franklin a few months before had suggested to Mr. Montagu in a letter which he received on the eve of his embarkation from England†, thus presenting to him a proof, brilliant and conclusive, that Lady Franklin's influence over me was irresistible, and that she had reckoned on its being so beforehand.

My decision as to the site put an end to the prolonged discussions on that subject, for I had given free scope to the expression of public opinion upon it, and found public opinion to be as various as the interests of the different localities. My own judgement was confirmed by the strong representations made to me in its favour by Mr. Gell, and by the then Archdeacon of Van Diemen's Land, my most faithful and attached friend and counsellor.

The site formed a small portion of a little farm of eighty acres belonging to the Government, about twenty miles from Hobart

---

* In my despatch to the Secretary of State I suggested that the valuable assistance of Dr. Arnold and of Dr. Peacock, Dean of Ely, should be requested for the framing of the Charter.

† This is the letter alluded to in a former page.

Town, easy of access both by land and water, on the skirts of a rural township or village, which had been one of the most zealous and the most liberal in its pecuniary subscriptions, yet secluded advantageously from the evils of the large towns. The farm, which was but little profitable, had been some years before ordered by the Colonial Office to be sold, but the execution of the order had been delayed, in consequence of my predecessor's representations, until farther instructions were received. The cottage residence upon it was extremely dilapidated, and was likely to remain so, since under these circumstances I did not feel myself justified in charging Her Majesty's Government with the expensive repairs which would be required to make it habitable. Such being the case, I considered that my successor in the government would receive compensation for the loss of the farm, if considered by Her Majesty's Government entitled to it*, and that it was desirable for me in the meantime to secure the land if possible from the crown for the purposes of the College. The Lieutenant-Governor has it not in his power to appropriate more than ten acres of land to any public purpose without the previous sanction of the Secretary of State. This portion of the farm therefore I set apart for the College, and requested from the Secretary of State the gift of the remainder. The first stone of the College was laid on the 6th of November 1840, in the presence of the Executive and Legislative Councils, of the heads of various departments, of the clergy, and of my friends Captains Ross and Crozier, and the officers of the ' Erebus' and ' Terror,' then about to sail from our shores to the Antarctic Ocean.

The College was dedicated to Christ : Himself the great Cornerstone of a building which was intended to train up christian youth in the faith as well as in the learning of christian gentle-

---

* It may not be irrelevant for me here to state, that in the year 1840, the Legislative Council voted an increase to the Lieutenant-Governor's salary, so as to make it amount to £4000 a year. I transmitted this vote to the Secretary of State, declining to recommend the Council's liberal vote to his lordship's acceptance in my own case, but recommending that it should be considered in that of my successor, since I had found that the present salary was totally inadequate to the expenditure required. I received from Lord John Russell an expression of his lordship's approbation of the "spirit" in which my sentiments on this subject had been conveyed to him.

At the first meeting of the Legislative Council after the arrival of Sir Eardley Wilmot, a similar vote of the Council was again passed, and received the sanction of Lord Stanley.

men, and the prayer of the late excellent and revered Archdeacon Hutchins invoked a blessing on our work. (See Appendix E.)

Mr. Montagu had not at this time returned to the colony; he did not arrive until early in the following year. I soon perceived that the College did not meet with his approbation. Mr. Montagu's objections to it however would have given way, if he could have persuaded me to change the site of the building to the immediate neighbourhood of Hobart Town, on or adjoining to the property of Mr. Swanston, and such was Mr. Montagu's estimate of his own or Mr. Swanston's influence in that neighbourhood, that he pledged himself to procure a subscription of 4000*l.* if I would effect this change. It may be easily concluded, after all that I have stated above, that such a proposition could not be entertained by me for a moment. Mr. Montagu's hostility to it became more undisguised, he opposed more than the *vis inertiæ* to the erection of the buildings, and when the time arrived that it was no longer worth his while to conceal his hostility to my government and his thorough disaffection to myself, the 'Van Diemen's Land Chronicle' gave a transcript of his sentiments which all his friends as well as foes could recognise.

Mr. Montagu was so well aware that he thwarted my wishes and endeavours for the establishment of the College in Van Diemen's Land, and he has at the same time such indubitable proof that my wishes on this subject were warmly and anxiously participated in by Lady Franklin, that the conclusion seems to him highly plausible, that hence arose one of the reasons for his suspension. It suited his purpose to present this aspect of the matter to Lord Stanley, if I may credit his own testimony in his book, and this is why I deem it necessary to enter into this explanation.

I may be excused perhaps for adding, that Lady Franklin's intention of contributing to the endowment of the College gave her a personal concern in its success. This intention was scarcely known to any but her own family; but the last act of Lady Franklin in Van Diemen's Land was, to make over 400 acres of land which she had purchased, in the neighbourhood of Hobart Town, with a small museum erected on it, into the hands of trustees* for the benefit of a future college. The endowment

---

* It was originally intended by Lady Franklin that the Tasmanian Society of Natural History should be the trustees of this property, but as that body

was not made to the favourite foundation at New Norfolk, for over this the shadows of annihilation had already fallen, but to any collegiate institution whatever which might be founded in Van Diemen's Land with the approbation of the bishop of the diocese for twenty years to come; and in default of any such foundation at the end of that period, to the improvement of the existing schools of the colony at the discretion of the trustees.

Having entered with more detail than I intended into this transaction, I shall not discuss any other points upon which I had to protect my wife against Mr. Montagu's calumnies. The main charge (that of being the cause of his suspension), to which all the others were subservient,—without which they were all good for nothing, was evidently one which could not stand against my full and flat contradiction. Accordingly I gave to the Secretary of State my unqualified contradiction to this statement of Mr. Montagu.

In transmitting to Lord Stanley the substance of the foregoing pages respecting the disclosures of Mr. Montagu's book, I could not but call his lordship's attention to the nature of the unequal contest in which I had been engaged; and if, in characterizing Mr. Montagu's policy and pointing out the evils attendant upon the abandonment of the Governor by the minister whom he had looked to for support, I expressed myself with a freedom and warmth not usually characteristic of official despatches, it was that the occasion called for it, and that I wrote under a deep sense of injury. I did not forget the respect due to my official superior, nor has Lord Stanley accused me of doing so. To have made my representations in private rather than officially and in a straightforward way, was not according to my notions either of duty or decorum, and would have been a great injustice to myself, which I was not called upon to commit. The evil had been already done,—it was public, and I rejoiced that while still in the seat of authority, it had pleased God to afford me the means of recording, in the archives of that colony which had witnessed the injuries and insults to which a

had no legal or chartered existence, and was moreover threatened with extinction when I left Van Diemen's Land, this part of her wishes could be no further carried into effect than by making complimentary mention of them in the deed, and selecting the trustees from their number. Some circumstances which occurred in Van Diemen's Land, shortly before my departure, induce me to be thus minute.

governor might be exposed when the shield of Her Majesty's government was no longer interposed to protect him, the defence which truth and a good conscience, that armour of proof, had enabled me to make.

In the despatches deposited in those archives, my successors may read that I defended the honour of my office, and pledged myself to leave no lawful means untried for the full exposure of the system of intrigues and misrepresentations by which Lord Stanley had been deceived, and his apparent sanction obtained for the injury of my character and the degradation of my government. I assured his lordship that I believed this to be my appointed path of duty.

My principal despatch on this subject bears date the 19th of July 1843; it was accompanied or followed by several others illustrative of particular facts. One of these transmitted to Lord Stanley the published copy before alluded to of his lordship's despatch (No. 150) as contained in the 'Hobart Town Courier' of the 7th of July.

In the despatch conveying this publication, I submitted to his lordship, that had he thought fit to remove me from my office at the time that he transmitted the original, I should have had little ground of complaint, though, now deeply as ever, and even more than ever impressed with the justness and necessity of my act of suspension, the good effects of which were proved by the quiet and healthy state of the colony ; but that since an imperative sense of duty had prevented me from abruptly throwing up my government in disgust, I felt myself entitled, until I could receive Lord Stanley's decision upon my conditional resignation, to the protection due to my office, and still more was the community entitled to the protection of the government from the evils attendant on the unbridled triumph of an adverse and agitating faction.

The despatch at the beginning of this narrative was published in all the newspapers of the colony at this particular moment, in order to prove that Lord Stanley and the writer of the ' book' held the same sentiments. It was evident that I was left in the seat of little better than nominal government, while the Colonial Secretary, whom I had dismissed from office, was in possession of the unlimited confidence of the Secretary of State, a position of which there cannot be a doubt that Mr. Montagu possessed the talent to take a full advantage.

I gave to Lord Stanley another presumptive instance of the influence of the family compact as it was boastfully exhibited in Van Diemen's Land at this period.

The 'Colonial Times' newspaper of the 25th of July (1843) informed the public, that by a ship just arrived (the Jane), which sailed on the 18th of March, information had been received that Lord Stanley refused to recognise my removal of Mr. Forster from the Probation Department (see page 42), and that he was to be reinstated forthwith. The 'Courier' of the 28th of July repeated the same intelligence with the additional information, that Mr. Forster was also to be appointed Comptroller-general of Convicts, an appointment which might be expected immediately to supersede that to which he was to be reinstated, and which Lord Stanley had himself told me would be filled by an officer who was to be sent out from England*. (See page 54.) The source of this information could not be doubted, for on the morning of the very same day on which the 'Colonial Times,' an evening paper, came out, Mr. Forster had received a private letter from a Department in Downing-street, informing him that he was to be reinstated in the office of Director-general of the Probation System, a department, it may be observed, which was no longer in existence. Mr. Forster had himself made a communication

---

* The following is the passage from the 'Courier.' It forms the leading article :—

"Our readers will not be surprised to hear that Dr. Milligan, as ' Inspector of the Department of Convict Discipline,' has not been confirmed by Lord Stanley. Advices have already been received, by which it is understood that the Secretary of State for the Colonies no sooner had intelligence of this strange appointment, than he issued instructions to reverse the Lieut.-Governor's decree, and to reinstate Mr. Forster in the post for which he is acknowledged to be so eminently qualified. Although this announcement has not yet been officially received, we are enabled positively to state that such is the fact. Mr. Forster is to resume immediately his duties as Chief Police Magistrate† and Director of the Probation Department. Upon the arrival of Sir Eardley Wilmot, who stands pledged to embark from England on or before the 1st of April, and may therefore daily be expected, Mr. Burgess will relieve Mr. Forster as his successor to the office of Chief Police Magistrate. This gentleman, who we hear is a barrister, will accompany our new Lieut.-Governor. Mr. Forster has been chosen by Lord Stanley to hold a responsible office under the new system, as Comptroller-general of Convicts, with a salary of 1000l. per annum, with 200l. allowed for travelling expenses and other contingencies. Mr. Milligan returns whence he came, if any one knows where that is."—*Courier*, July 28, 1843.

Allusion to the same event is made at an earlier date, the 14th of July, in 'Murray's Review.'

---

† Of this he had never been deprived.

to this effect to Mr. Bicheno, the Colonial Secretary, for my information.

The communication was a startling one, for when the 'Jane' left England on the 18th of March, my despatch reporting the change I had effected in Mr. Forster's position, and the reasons for it, had not yet arrived there, so that if Lord Stanley had really come to the decision referred to, it must have been upon private, ex-parte and unauthorized information, a course which appeared to me incredible, unless his lordship had yielded to the influence of some such delusive misrepresentations as those which I had reason to believe had already prevailed in his lordship's office.

Moreover the assurance his lordship had given me in his despatch of the 25th of November 1842 (No. 175), that the Comptroller-general would be sent out from England, was one which I felt to be of considerable importance to the colony, and I had understood that it was in that light his lordship regarded it. I should therefore at once have concluded that Mr. Forster's informant had been misled, had I not lately witnessed so many remarkable instances, that official information from that quarter (I mean the quarter of Mr. Forster and Mr. Montagu's correspondents) might always be trusted to, especially in cases where the exhibition of Mr. Montagu's paramount influence at the Colonial Office was the object intended; and had it not been for this fact, I should have deemed it unnecessary, as I respectfully submitted to Lord Stanley in my despatch of the 29th of July, to press upon his lordship the justice of suspending his judgement upon any case connected with the colony and with my government, until he was in possession of the entire statements belonging to it.

The above was the last I think of the Downing-street bulletins issued in Van Diemen's Land during the short remaining term of my government. I waited to see the result of this.

But I had still another duty to perform in justice to myself.

It was not to be supposed that the affairs of that vast colonial empire over which Lord Stanley presides could receive in their minutiæ his lordship's attention. It was evident that the capacity of no one man could enter into the particulars of all the various cases which are daily brought before his lordship from every quarter of the globe, and thus that a division of labour recognized by the government no less than by every principle of justice, must of necessity be established in his lordship's department. Such were the reasons, expressed in nearly these words, which I respectfully submitted to Lord Stanley as my apology for believing that he had probably delegated to inferior officers the examination of Mr. Montagu's case.

Amongst these subordinate officers, I knew Mr. Montagu to have personal and intimate friends; I also knew that it was his avowed policy always to ingratiate himself with the subordinates in office in order the better to gain the ear of the chief; and further I was aware, that no means had been left untried by Mr. Montagu to collect from all quarters in his favour, a weight of influence difficult to resist, and to give to his serviceable talents an importance, which, at the juncture referred to, was likely to be more than duly appreciated*.

* The following fact is an illustration of these positions.

Previous to the interruption of all amicable relations between Mr. Montagu and myself, it became known that the Acting Clerk of the Councils, Mr. Nairn, would have to relinquish his situation in consequence of arrangements from home. Under these circumstances I had in view the offering him the only vacant situation then at my disposal, when Mr. Montagu represented to me that the office of Assistant Colonial Secretary would in all probability soon become vacant by the resignation of Mr. Mitchell, and that there was no one whom he considered better fitted to fill it than Mr. Nairn, nor any one whom he should prefer to him. These views recommended themselves to me on account of Mr. Nairn's capacity and knowledge of affairs, and because he had entered official life in Mr. Montagu's office under my government, and been trained under Mr. Montagu's eye. To Mr. Nairn, Mr. Montagu made similar representations, with the additional proposal that he (Mr. Nairn) should return immediately to the Colonial Secretary's office, where he had no doubt I would sanction his receiving an immediate salary of 250*l.* a year, waiting the vacancy of the superior office.

Within a month after Mr. Montagu's embarkation for England the anticipated vacancy occurred, and Mr. Nairn, then out of employment, received from me the appointment of Assistant Colonial Secretary under Mr. Boyes. I also reported the appointment with strong recommendations to the Secretary of State.

In the same ship in which Mr. Montagu took his passage to England was a young man of good family and connexions, who had been some little time in the Colony for the purpose of learning farming, and was going home, not intending, I believe, to return.

To this gentleman Mr. Montagu addressed himself, informed him that the place of Assistant Colonial Secretary was about to become vacant, advised him to apply for it without delay, enhanced its actual value, and in short induced Mr. Seymour to make up his mind to another antipodean voyage as quickly as possible, should he succeed in the application to the Colonial Office, which on Mr. Montagu's representations he determined to make.

The result of that application is well known. Mr F. Seymour returned to the colony in company with Mr. Bicheno in 1843, as Assistant Colonial Secretary, and then learnt for the first time, that the person he had superseded

An absent man, and one who disdained to obtain from the private sympathies of his judge, if he could have presumed upon doing so, what was due only to justice and truth, was likely to be sensitive to the consequences of so unequal a position. Having then, with more honesty than discretion perhaps, expressed my conclusions from these facts, I entreated of Lord Stanley that he would, either in his own person or by the assistance of individuals unconnected with Mr. Montagu or with Van Diemen's Land, thoroughly investigate the whole of the circumstances which had transpired in reference to Mr. Montagu since the period of his suspension.

It was clear that at this period I believed Lord Stanley had been unconsciously deceived by Mr. Montagu, and that I had in his lordship's candour and justice implicit trust. Though I knew that the personal consideration of all the documents to which I referred him must involve a considerable amount of labour, I ventured to express my conviction that I should be doing his lordship great injustice did I suppose that such a consideration would weigh with him when a higher and a sacred duty was in the balance. I marked this despatch " confidential," (it met, alas! with the fate of many other despatches so distinguished,) and sent a copy of it to my friend Sir James Ross, with a request that he would deliver it personally into the hands of Lord Stanley, a commission which Sir James Ross lost no time in executing.

In about the second week, I believe, in July, I read in the ' Times ' newspaper of the 24th of February, the Gazette notice of Sir Eardley Wilmot's appointment to the government of Van Diemen's Land,—an announcement which, however securely I had been looking to my release from the cares of government, could not but cause me some surprise, for I had as yet received no notice from the Colonial Office on the subject, and it was natural for me to conclude, that, as in the case of my predecessor,

---

was the faithful and long-tried clerk of Mr. Montagu, for whom that gentleman had first bespoken my future appointment, and whom he had afterwards taken active means to supplant.

It is no disparagement to the talents and application of Mr. Seymour, of whom, from personal knowledge, I have formed the most favourable opinion, to say, that having had no previous official training or experience, I found it necessary, on the representation of Mr. Bicheno, the new Colonial Secretary, to place him under an apprenticeship for about two months to Mr. Nairn. Thus I had to retain the services of these two gentlemen for the same office, the one at whole, the other at half salary.

several months would be granted me for settling my affairs, both public and private, before the arrival of my successor. This conclusion was the more inevitable, because the Colonial Secretary, who arrived in April, had not, as I have already stated, been authorized to make any communication to me indicative of an approaching change.

There were at this time only two vessels in the harbour bound eventually and direct for England, it being that season of the year (the Australian winter) when the wool exports are not ready, and when few passengers with families undertake, but from necessity, a voyage which must bring them off the English coast in the stormy season.

Of these vessels, one only was suited to my purpose. She was about to sail for Sydney with an English cargo, and was then to repair to Port Phillip to take in the first wool-cargo that presented itself, and be ready to sail at the close of the year or the beginning of the next.

I detained this vessel, by the kindness of the captain, a couple of days, in order to get some of my heavy baggage on board, and engaged a passage in her for myself and my family from Port Phillip, to which place it would thus be necessary for me to repair at a fixed period.

Woful were the countenances of the Derwent Bank clique, when they found that not even the announcement of the impending arrival of my successor could scare me from my post. It was expected by them that the Gazette notice in the 'Times' would have served me instead of a despatch; but perceiving that I was of a different opinion, they foresaw that I should be still on the spot when Sir Eardley Wilmot arrived; and then, what disclosures! what warnings! The virtuous indignation excited at my immoveability knew no bounds!

The organs of the sentiments of this party teemed with the most ludicrous exhibitions of disappointment and rage; whispered threats of what was to happen when the ægis of my governor's commission could no longer shield me from the terrors of the law, were made to reach my ears. Emissaries were employed to arouse if possible the timid misgivings of members of my family, and even kind and well-meaning friends, knowing the unprincipled audacity of a few of the understrappers of this party, brought before me the possibility of their venturing to bring some fabricated legal case against me, for the pure sake of annoyance, as soon as I had resigned the government. I was assured by these friends, in order to reconcile me to this view of things, that my predecessor could not with impunity have ventured on the step I was contemplating*.

Notwithstanding,—the two ships left the harbour, the one for England, the other for Sydney, and still, Government-house retained its occupants. The case grew desperate in the eyes of those who were so anxious that it should be ready swept and cleaned for Sir Eardley Wilmot.

I took the first opportunity that presented itself at a public meeting, to allude to the approaching change in the administration of the government; but my post was still, according to my old-fashioned notions, on the deck of my vessel. I was waiting for orders, and recognised none but those of my chief.

In the meantime, under the impression that my recall despatch would certainly precede by a considerable interval the actual arrival of my successor, I was preparing for settlement in the Legislative Council, already adjourned beyond the ordinary period, a measure which I deemed of the utmost importance.

Had Lord Stanley's most valuable and masterly despatch, if I may be permitted so to characterise it, enclosing a letter to the late Dr. Arnold, on the grant of a royal charter for the College, been brought before the Legislative Council at this period according to my intention, I have little doubt that it would have recommended itself to that body, and thus, that a measure which for four years had occupied the public mind would at last have been accomplished. I had solicited this charter soon after the arrival of the Principal of the College, and had subsequently pressed it on the consideration of the Secretary of State. Lord Stanley now held out the promise of the desired boon on certain conditions, the consideration of which I thought it right to defer till the arrival, first of the new Colonial Secretary, and then of the Bishop of Tasmania, whose opinions, as a new and important element in the judgement to be formed, it was most desirable to obtain. The subject was now under discussion in the Executive Council, of which the Bishop is a member, and,

---

* My predecessor does not appear to have participated in the fears entertained for him, if I may judge from a letter which he had the kindness to leave for me at Government-house, and in which he appears to have contemplated at one time the receiving me on my arrival, which was later than was expected.

on the 17th of August it was decided, that at the following meeting, the opinions of the members should be finally expressed upon the propositions of the Secretary of State.

On the evening of that day Sir Eardley Wilmot landed on an unfrequented part of the coast, from the 'Cressy' prison-ship which had mistaken the entrance of the port, and on the following night he entered Hobart Town. He brought me no communication from Lord Stanley as to his appointment, and no explanation of the anomaly. On Sunday the 20th however, the 'Gilmore' prison-ship arrived, and conveyed to me the duplicate of a despatch from the Secretary of State, announcing to me the appointment of a successor in the government of the colony, and on Monday the 21st, I received by the 'Eamont' merchantman the original of the despatch, bearing date the 10th of February, in which his lordship signified his pleasure on this subject.

Of this recall-despatch I shall say but little. That Lord Stanley should call to mind at the last moment that the person he addressed had lawfully represented the Queen's authority in the place to which he was appointed, and, unless convicted of misdeeds, was entitled to the ordinary acknowledgements of his faithful services, was, under all the circumstances I have related, scarcely perhaps to be expected. It could not " be too distinctly understood," in the case of Mr. Montagu, that he " retired from the situation he had so long filled, with his hold on the respect and confidence of Her Majesty's Government undiminished." The inferior officer thus complimented, what terms remained for the Governor?

The despatch, in civil language, was to the effect, that my term of service having expired, I must be expecting my discharge, and a hope was politely expressed, that the term of six weeks or two months, which it was expected would elapse before my supersession, would be sufficient for my convenience.

On the day when the original of the despatch arrived, Sir Eardley Wilmot took the oaths of office. I remained still ten days longer in Government-house, being unable, in spite of the exertion of the utmost diligence, to remove my family and dispose of my effects in less time. During this period Sir Eardley Wilmot resided with the Colonial Secretary and paid a visit to Launceston, where there is an official residence.

The above events were reported by me to Lord Stanley in a despatch, dated from Government-house on the day I resigned the government. I expressed in it my trust that the speedy arrival of Sir Eardley Wilmot after his appointment, without any announcement or timely notice, contrary to his lordship's intention as expressed in his despatch, would be an ample apology, if any were wanting, for not having anticipated his lordship's wishes, and sooner prepared for the vacation of my office, and I regretted the embarrassment which had thus been caused, on my successor's account as well as my own. It appeared to me the result of wilfulness or great negligence in some inferior branch of his lordship's department, where it must have been well-known, I conceived, that the ship by which the original despatch was transmitted was one not fitted for the conveyance of any speedy missive. It had been on some former occasion, when despatches were unusually detained, represented as such at the Colonial Office,—" a notoriously slow sailer." On the present occasion the ship put back and was detained for six weeks in Ireland, whilst no care was taken to send the duplicate by the intervening opportunities prior to the sailing of the ' Gilmore,' an official irregularity which could not fail to strike me forcibly. Had the despatch arrived at the time intended by the Secretary of State, I should have had a short six weeks' notice of the arrival of my successor.

The " notoriously slow sailer" was a weak point in my remonstrance upon the unbecoming mode of my recall; it certainly savoured more of the Captain than of the Governor, and when, in the interview with which I was honoured on my return to England, Lord Stanley condescended to point it out to me, I at once abandoned it.

It must be recollected, however, that as the Governor also, I had some reason to be sensitive as to the sailing qualities of despatch-bearing ships, since it was the unusually long passage of a vessel bearing my despatch and reports on convict discipline in November 1842 which subjected me to the observation of Lord Stanley, when he had decided upon overturning my arrangements, that it was desirable that I should have given him earlier information on that subject.

My despatch upon the late events, dated from Government-house, 21st August, with a few observations to which they gave rise, was not closed until after an interval of two or three weeks, when I was living as a private individual, in the midst of the people over whom I had been so lately presiding, in the house of the Brigade-Major, which he had kindly vacated for my convenience. It was one of the many hospitable homes which the kindness of my friends placed at my disposal*. Here, surrounded by friends, and greeted in public with more outward demonstrations of respect than even in the days of my government, I remained for two months, busily occupied, having yet two or three months more before me, ere the 'Rajah,' in which I had engaged my passage, would complete her cargo at Port Phillip.

It was in the house of the Brigade-Major, as well as in Government-house during the short period which intervened between my successor's landing and my vacation of that residence, that I received the numerous and kind addresses which were presented to me on my retirement from the government. They have been placed in the Colonial Office, and are also in the hands of my friends both here and in Van Diemen's Land. Of these addresses I will merely say, that they were the results, not of the hole-and-corner combinations of personal adherents and partisans, but of public meetings, convened in almost every case after my successor's arrival. To this fact I attribute one element of their value. They were addressed to me after I had retired from the government, when those who wrote and adopted them could no longer, to use the language of one of these documents, be influenced by fear or favour, in the presence of a new Governor, and in the face of a blighting faction, always ready by sneers or by bullying to wither or to crush the expression of any sentiment but its own.

That the writers and the signers of them, who amounted to many thousands, may have felt that my six or seven years' go-

---

* The scurrilous and mendacious articles in 'Murray's Review' on this occasion were alluded to in terms highly flattering to myself in a professional London journal, which was probably not aware that the fictions of the Van Diemen's Land editor are too well-known in the colony to need refutation, or which at any rate considered that they might admit of exposure elsewhere. The article in the United Service Gazette was sent out to Van Diemen's Land and produced a *plat réchauffé* from Mr. Murray, garnished with fresh ornaments and seasoned with condiments to relieve its staleness.

I owe the knowledge of this otherwise unimportant fact to the kindness of a valued friend of mine, a staff officer of the 51st regiment, who sent me Mr. Murray's story with his own marginal comments, accompanied by a letter in which he expresses his regret that such "abominable untruths should have the *semblance* even of confirmation by appearing in a newspaper daring to try and connect them with the 51st regiment," whose well-known sentiments of regard and respect he appeals to as a sufficient assurance to me, if I needed such, " of the contempt and abhorrence felt on this occasion by himself and the rest of his brother-officers."

vernment of Van Diemen's Land had not altogether been free from error, (and who more conscious of this than myself?) I can scarcely doubt; that they may have felt that an abler hand would more easily have controlled the evil elements with which I had to contend, or a subtler intellect have turned them to its own political purposes, may be also true; yet with all these allowances, I am justified, I think, in believing that they will look back to my government of Van Diemen's Land, as one, the influence of which was for good and not for evil,—one which promoted the moral and religious interests of the colony, and did not neglect its economical welfare, though this was retarded (within a very recent period) by circumstances over which, as one of these addresses justly says, I had no control, and which have overwhelmed alike all the Australian colonies. I trust they will feel that it is a government which, had it been supported by the present Secretary of State for the Colonies, since the epoch of his accession to power, would have left permanent traces of its beneficial working.

It is painful to me thus to speak of myself; but I will venture to say,—I believe I have said it before,—that had not the colonists of Van Diemen's Land appreciated my endeavours for their good, and given me their esteem and confidence and support, it would not have been possible for me, abandoned as I was by the minister, and sacrificed to the intrigues of a party which had access to his ear, to have carried on my government.

I have yet one more fact to relate in illustration of this assertion.

Some pages back, when treating of the events of 1842, I stated that I had separated the administration of the Convict and Police Departments, which had been for the last twelvemonth experimentally united in the person of Mr. Forster.

The representations of Mr. Forster on this subject, notwithstanding the intimation conveyed to me by that officer of his intention to transmit them through my hands, the only legitimate channel, reached England before my own Report, but not before a despatch (previously alluded to) which I took particular pains should reach the Secretary of State in time to give him due notice of my intentions (see page 43). Without waiting however for the announced Report, or taking any notice of the announcement, but acting, as I was now informed by his lordship himself, in a despatch dated March 23, 1843*, on private information, Lord Stanley commands me to restore Mr. Forster immediately to the place of Director of the Probation Department†. The act which appeared to be commanded of me was not possible except by a fiction. It was not in Lord Stanley's power, any more than it was in his intention, to make the actual system of convict management fall back upon the old one of a year ago. He could not mean me to break up all the arrangements which had been made and were acted on, to meet the exigencies of accumulated bodies of convicts, to recall the prisoners sent into private service, to dismiss the board which regulated their distribution, and to crush all the growth of a system, which, when Mr. Forster administered the Probation Department, had not received its development. If his lordship had desired me to give Mr. Forster the same amount of labour he had in his former situation, though that amount I had considered too much for his convenient and adequate performance, or the same amount of salary, and to restore to him with these the same title, leaving the newly-grafted department, which embraced the secondary and subsequent stages of punishment, to be separately considered, such an arrangement, though a complicated and an uneconomical one, would have been intelligible and practicable. But I could not so understand my instructions. I was to remove Mr. Milligan, the officer who had been performing Mr. Forster's former duties, with the superadded ones involved in the extension of the department, and to put Mr. Forster in his place under the disguise of his old title, and

---

* Lord Stanley's despatch was marked " private." It is difficult to conjecture the intention of this designation, since the act commanded was a public one, and could not be made to appear in any other light than as the consequence of peremptory orders from the Colonial Office. And besides, the contents of his lordship's despatch were, as I have already stated, public property before the despatch itself arrived in the colony. The despatch was not even written until after the sailing of the ship which brought the private information. I refer the reader to the extract from the ' Courier' (page 81), where it will be seen that not only did that newspaper announce Mr. Forster's restoration, and his appointment to the Comptroller-generalship, but that this announcement on private information was expressly stated to be with the *knowledge that the official statement of it had not been received by the Lieutenant-Governor.* A more convincing proof could not be required of this premature information coming from the Colonial Office. That office alone could know and could communicate such a fact, as that the official despatch had not yet been sent.

† It must be borne in mind, that the restoration involved Mr. Forster's reoccupation of a double office.

thus, by the insertion of a few words in the Gazette, announcing Mr. Forster to be appointed Director of the Probation Department, proclaim to the colony that the new Department of Convict Discipline, which had superseded and absorbed it, the rules and appointments of this new department, and the officer administering it, were nothing more than shadows. To have done so would have been, in my view of things, to delude Lord Stanley and to stultify myself. I received his lordship's despatch by the same ship which brought my successor, and my timely recall (for such I must in the present instance consider it) relieved me from the very painful predicament in which I was placed; since, as I had the honour of submitting to Lord Stanley, so long as I administered the government, I could neither recognise the principle that my public acts, based on the most disinterested zeal for the public good, should be overturned by private and ex-parte representations in his lordship's office, nor could I consent to be the instrument of making known to the public the personal affront involved in the orders given to me.

The re-appointment of Mr. Forster bore the aspect of a mere gratuitous triumph, since the same despatch informs me that he would enter upon his duties merely as a *preparation* for those of Comptroller-general, which appointment was to be almost immediately expected (it arrived I think about a month after). It will be perceived that this was in direct contradiction to Lord Stanley's communication to me a few months before, that the Comptroller-general would be sent out from England.

The same appointment recognises that very division of the Convict and Police Departments, which for the sake apparently of a month's triumph to Mr. Forster, I was condemned for having effected. It is worthy of observation, that so well known beforehand was this result of Mr. Forster's means of private influence with the Colonial Office, or so thoroughly was it relied on, that the Hobart Town Almanac, a sheet published by Mr. Elliston of the 'Courier,' at the close of 1842, after all the changes I had made had been gazetted, recognises no such thing as the "Department of Convict Discipline," and no such person as Mr. Milligan, the administrator of it!

I could not hesitate to point out once more, humbly, but earnestly and faithfully, to Lord Stanley, the evil of these private influences in his lordship's office. Though my personal connexion with the colony had ceased, I had its interests deeply at heart, and could not contemplate without the greatest alarm, a system which placed it at the mercy of ex-parte and interested statements, veiled however, before they could be brought under Lord Stanley's consideration, in the specious garb of the public good. What governor, I respectfully submitted to Lord Stanley, could be safe, if, instead of being regarded as the *most* faithful, the *most* trustworthy, and the *most* disinterested of Her Majesty's servants in the colony he governs,—for such, viewing his awful responsibility, he at least ought to be,—he is treated inversely to his high functions and his station, and finds his own subordinate officers preferred before him? And if the governor, who is supposed to have the right of easy access to Her Majesty's Government, be not safe under such influences, how much less the private individual! It was this conviction, I added, pressing home to the feelings of every colonist, which made the case of the governor, in an instance like the present, the case of every man. I ventured to affirm, that the history of the home administration of this colony, since the period when Mr. Montagu first established himself in his lordship's confidence, was a practical commentary on those simple and obvious truths,—that the influence of a family compact was universally believed and openly discussed in the colony ; that in recent instances, the many deplored and the few triumphed in it. I trusted that if his lordship had thought fit hitherto to mistrust the representations which had been made to him on these sinister influences, he would listen to those of the Governor of a colony who closed his administration by entreating his consideration of the facts now submitted, and that he would perceive I spoke the language, not of wounded feeling alone, but of duty and respect to him and to his sovereign.

I am thus particular in noticing certain passages in my despatches and letters to Lord Stanley, not because I have any pleasure in repeating language which might perhaps have been subdued and curtailed with advantage, but because I wish my friends to be aware of the provocations, if they are to be considered such, which Lord Stanley has received from me. Yet I must do his lordship the justice to believe that the treatment I have received at his hands is neither owing to my homely, but never disrespectful language, nor to his entire disregard of the truths therein conveyed. I attribute his lordship's policy towards me to other causes.

It will be seen farther on, that my only answer to the remonstrance I respectfully transmitted to Lord Stanley on the transaction I have just alluded to, was, that his lordship does not think it necessary to discuss with me his appointments, &c.

To return for a moment to my instructions respecting Mr. Forster's restoration.

I was so impressed with the fatal consequences of this measure as affecting the just authority of the Governor and the dignity of his office, that in justice to Sir Eardley Wilmot, as well as to the meritorious officer who was to be unceremoniously ousted from his place, for no fault of his, I felt it to be my duty to represent to His Excellency my opinions, and to suggest that a short delay would probably bring the appointment of Mr. Forster to be Comptroller-general, and thus necessarily supersede, with the introduction of the new system of convict discipline, all existing arrangements.

I felt convinced that such a compromise would be acceptable even to Lord Stanley, since his lordship would probably not have sent me the instructions he did send, had he been aware how irreconcilable they were to existing institutions, and that he would probably regret those instructions when he read my explanatory despatch on the changes, of which, under mistaken views, he had now disapproved. Sir Eardley Wilmot agreed with me in this view of things, but he was immediately after induced to change his opinion, and the very next day I believe, or the following one, Mr. Milligan, at a few hours' notice, was dismissed from his office; like a discomfited usurper, and Mr. Forster slid glibly and comfortably into it. He found everything ready to his hand, the machinery in good order, the wheels well-oiled, every officer at his post, understanding well his business. The whole affair was more like the sleight-of-hand exhibition of the conjuring art, than the serious result of the Secretary of State's deliberations. In the Gazette announcement, not the slightest notice was taken of the ex-Inspector of Convict Discipline, or of the department which he had with great diligence organized. It was simply announced that Mr. Forster was appointed Director-general of the Probation System. He was so gazetted, unconditionally, for the first time; for it must be recollected that Mr. Forster's original appointment to this office proceeded from me, and not from the Secretary of State, and that his lordship's confirmation of it had not been received; yet neither this circumstance, nor the fact that, being an experimental measure*, it was liable to revision according to the results of its working, was of any avail in favour of my just influence with the Secretary of State, when the interests of Mr. Forster were in the balance. Undoubtedly the trial had lasted a shorter time than I had anticipated, for it had already convinced me, that to give to the chief Police Magistrate of the colony, who is, or was, by virtue of his office, a member also of the Executive Council, the farther control of the Convict Department, was to accumulate in his person an undue and unsafe degree of patronage and power. It would have been a great weakness in me, with these convictions, to have been stopped from doing what on this and on other no less important grounds, I thought right, because Mr. Forster was the relation and the friend of Mr. Montagu. I was well aware of all that would be urged on this score and on others against the changes I made in Mr. Forster's position, but these considerations did not weigh with me one jot, when the path of my duty was plain before me.

To the Secretary of State I gave no other reason for withdrawing from Mr. Forster the charge of the Probation Department, than those which, in language as little disagreeable to Mr. Forster's feelings as I could command, I had already addressed to himself. The reasons I gave were more than sufficient to prove the justice and necessity of my decision†.

It may be satisfactory to my friends in Van Diemen's Land to know that I explained my views on this head to Sir Eardley Wilmot, and strongly advised His Excellency, under the operation of the new system, to be jealous of delegating his patronage even as regarded the most subordinate appointments.

With these exceptions, which my sense of duty urged me

* In my minute to the Executive Council, May 20th 1841, I state that "in submitting my views to Her Majesty's Government, I shall request the continuance of this arrangement (viz. Mr. Forster's charge of the Probation department) may be contingent upon my future reports as to its efficiency." The minutes of the Executive Council are regularly transmitted to the Secretary of State.

† The propriety of the changes I had effected in the administration of this department was best exemplified by the results. There was perhaps no period in which the convicts were under better control than that which extended from the introduction of the above changes to the close of my government, and certainly none in which the colonists were better satisfied with the advantages to be derived from convict labour. I have already stated that a considerable saving to Her Majesty's Government was also effected.

to make, I refrained from having any communication with my successor as to the state of party-feeling, the character and conduct of individuals, the scandalous intrigues which had been recently practised, or my own grievances at Lord Stanley's hands. It was quite sufficient for me to have these things to relate to Lord Stanley himself; and besides, the peculiar delicacy of the position in which I found myself placed, as the survivor of my government on the spot where I had administered it, forbad my taking advantage of the circumstance to the prejudice of others. By so abstaining, however, I denied myself some explanations which the justice a man owes to himself might otherwise have led me to desire. These principles and explanations I also laid before Lord Stanley.

On the 3rd of November, 1843, I embarked with my family from Hobart Town, amidst a burst of generous and enthusiastic feeling, which, much as I had confided in the attachment of the people of Van Diemen's Land, could not but surprise, as well as deeply affect me. It was a day never to be forgotten by myself or by any one member of my family*.

Having freighted a vessel for the accommodation of myself and party, among whom I had the pleasure of including my esteemed friend the Bishop of Tasmania, we first visited a settlement of respectable free agriculturists, on the banks of the Huon river. Here, located upon land belonging to my wife, upon terms which were to enable them to become shortly the independent possessors of it, they had hewed themselves an opening in the dense forests which clothe the banks of that river, and had laid its soil open to the sun. In the rustic wooden chapel of this settlement, which is accessible only by water, or by a foot-track through the " bush," the Bishop administered for the first time the sacraments of our church to the inhabitants of the Huon forests. Proceeding to the entrance of Bass Strait, on our way towards Launceston, a gale obliged us to take shelter under Swan Island, one of two sites I had fixed upon for the erection of

---

* A faithful account of the kind feelings elicited by my departure from the shores of Van Diemen's Land, both on the northern and southern sides of the island, was given in the ' Hobart Town Advertiser,' November 7, 1843, and in the ' Launceston Examiner,' November 18, 1843.

lighthouses, necessary for the safe navigation of Bass Strait, and for which I had obtained the sanction of the Secretary of State. On landing, I was requested to lay the first stone of the building. On Goose Island we found the lighthouse completed, and the officer who had been appointed to its charge residing there, but the lanterns had not yet arrived. We then proceeded to Flinder's Island, the dwelling-place of the sole remnant of the Aborigines of Van Diemen's Land, now scarcely exceeding fifty souls, including some half-castes. A few of the younger members of this interesting black family were baptized by the Bishop, who promised himself another pastoral visit to them.

Entering the port of George Town and anchoring there, a signal was made to Launceston, and a deputation from that town, according to previous arrangement, waited on me on board my schooner, and presented me with an address signed by the most respectable inhabitants of the town and district on my retirement from the government.

I quitted the Tamar with the conviction that I had left some of my most estimable and attached friends in that district, and here also I parted from the Bishop, who having intended to continue his pastoral visit with me to Circular Head, found himself unexpectedly obliged to return to his more urgent duties at Hobart Town.

Circular Head is the head-quarters of the Van Diemen's Land Company's Agricultural Establishment. Situated at the northwest part of the island, remote from other settlements, it has for many years planted its own population on the soil, and existed almost as a little colony of itself. It is now rapidly, and, I trust, successfully, extending its operations.

From the officers of the Company resident here, I met with every kind attention. During the successive years of my government of Van Diemen's Land, I had never before been able to visit this spot; it was the last on which I set foot in Van Diemen's Land. We quitted its shores, probably for ever, on the 29th of November, and crossed over to Portland Bay, whence, after visiting the magnificent pasture lands in the interior, we sailed for Port Phillip. The ' Rajah ' had not yet taken in all her cargo, and six weeks more elapsed before she was ready to sail, though the season here is generally a little in advance of Van Diemen's Land, and she was one of the first ships which left the harbour. Our time was divided between a residence at an hotel in Melbourne and some excursions into the interior.

During all this time we were deeply indebted to the kind attention and valuable assistance and companionship of my valued friend Mr. La Trobe, the excellent and able Superintendent or Deputy-Governor of Port Phillip.

Finally, on the 10th of January 1844, we embarked on board the 'Rajah,' and commenced our homeward voyage by the westward passage, one which is frequently taken by vessels at the commencement of the season, when the westerly winds have not yet become permanent.

These details are wholly unimportant, and to say the truth, I have no other object in giving them but to afford my readers a little breathing-time in my narrative.

From George Town in Van Diemen's Land, I had transmitted to Lord Stanley an account of my departure and about a dozen or more addresses, received from various public bodies and from different districts of the island. On leaving its shores, I believed that for a time I had left all annoying subjects behind, but I was destined to meet the Secretary of State and his lordship's despatches again even in the course of my voyage home. The 'Rajah' arrived in due time at St. Helena, and here the first thing I learnt was, that Lord Stanley's already notorious despatch, No. 150, had arrived fresh from Cape Town, where it had just been published in the colonial journals. Nothing more natural I thought, considering that the despatch had been published by Mr. Montagu's friends in the Van Diemen's Land journals in July, and that Mr. Montagu was now, in the month of March, living at the Cape. In the intervening period it had been sent to the London 'Morning Herald,' where it appeared with a sort of apologetic heading in praise of Lord Stanley's intolerance of cruelty and injustice, of which what followed was to be the illustration.

The remaining part of my story must be quickly told. I landed at Portsmouth on the 6th of June 1844, and immediately transmitted to Lord Stanley a letter written at sea, which related to the St. George's Church case,—a case which had formed the crowning-point of Mr. Montagu's triumphant exculpation.

Subsequently to my transmission of the statements, upon

which Lord Stanley had formed his decision in this case, I had, at two or three different periods transmitted to his lordship documents, as they came into my possession, in further illustration of the positions advanced; and in particular in my despatch No. 95 (19th July 1843), I reported to him the discovery of the lost authority, which had hitherto baffled my most diligent search. The circumstances attending the production of this document were so remarkable, that I had deemed it desirable to submit them to the consideration of the Executive Council, since the members of that council and the whole colony had read in Lord Stanley's despatch No. 150, that Mr. Montagu was "entitled to be completely absolved of the fault imputed to him, and had repelled it to his lordship's entire satisfaction." Moreover it was an act of justice to Captain Cheyne, the accuracy of whose statements was established by the discovery of the document. The deliberations of the council and my own investigations were arrested however by the abrupt termination of my government in consequence of the sudden arrival of Sir Eardley Wilmot, but not before the council had had the fullest evidence that there had been "foul play" in the former suppression of the document, that every possible resistance had been offered to its present production, and that it was Mr. Montagu, and not myself, who gave the authority for the altered plans of the church. I forwarded the minutes of council and other necessary documents to Lord Stanley, with a copy of the authority given by Mr. Montagu. (See Appendix.)

On arriving in London, and going to the Colonial Office to leave a note for Lord Stanley in which I reported my return and requested the honour of an interview with his lordship, a letter which appeared to have been waiting my arrival was instantly put into my hands.

The reader who has had the patience to follow me through the preceding pages may perhaps feel interest enough in the result, to form to himself some anticipation of the contents of a letter thus meeting me half-way in my approach to the source, as I conceived, of justice and redress.

He will speculate whether it was a general acknowledgement of the series of despatches yet unanswered, which I had addressed to his lordship subsequent to the receipt of that which forms the text of this pamphlet, with a gracious assurance that they had all been carefully considered, and should be fairly and freely discussed, or whether it was a prefatory explanation of the untoward circumstances attending my recall, or a satisfactory acknowledgement of my recent letter on the St. George's Church case, or an answer to some one or other of those earnest yet respectful remonstrances which I had addressed to Lord Stanley on points on which he was now aware that I had been deeply aggrieved. There was abundant room for selection. It might be an expression of his lordship's regret at the manner in which I had understood the despatch No. 150, and at the use which had been made of it, and of his lordship's opinion that the conduct of Mr. Montagu and his adherents respecting the ' book ' was not to be defended; perhaps an assurance of satisfaction with the explanation I had been called on to make on the assertion of an abusive newspaper, or even a dignified admission that it was to be regretted my announced despatches on an important public measure, which had been overturned on the private representations of Mr. Forster, had not been waited for; perhaps an approving acknowledgement of my Reports on Convict Discipline, even though they had arrived too late for his lordship's use; or, at all events, a cordial assurance that the omission of all the usual expressions of approbation on my retirement from my government was by no means intended for censure, and admitted of being amply supplied.

No such conciliatory measure awaited me. The Secretary of State disdained the easy reparation even of wrongs which he had not intended, or in which he had no immediate part; but his lordship did not disdain to place himself in the attitude of the offended person, whilst at the same time he informed me that he did not think it consistent with the relative position held by himself and by me in Her Majesty's service to take notice of my charges and insinuations, and that he would not make to his subordinate officer, explanations which he owed to Her Majesty the Queen and to Parliament alone. His lordship had not so reasoned on the claims of a subordinate officer, when he preferred Mr. Montagu to me.

The observations I have quoted are addressed to my successor Sir Eardley Wilmot, in a despatch dated 31st January 1844, under cover to myself. In this Lord Stanley has taken the pains to cull from a series of despatches and letters written during the last few months of my government and subsequent residence in Van Diemen's Land, all the passages reflecting on the conduct of his lordship's office, by which my government had been so seriously embarrassed. The character of these selected passages may be pretty correctly ascertained by the epitome of them exhibited in the foregoing pages; and if, when withdrawn from the context which modifies them, and made to stand apart from the facts of which they are the commentary and the moral, they present a somewhat startling array, the cause should be looked for, not in the presumption of him who had at different periods felt it his duty to make these reflections, but in the stubborn truths and singular circumstances which had forced them upon me.

But Lord Stanley is pleased to overlook the facts I brought forward, and as if no illustrations whatever had been given of the observations I had respectfully submitted to him, his lordship, as the champion of the subordinate members of his office, against whom, he observes, the charges would appear to be directed, calls upon me for some specific statements. My statements I thought had been specific enough, but it was clear to me that Lord Stanley's intention was at once to shift my position from that of a complainant to that of a defendant, and to make it a personal, and therefore an embarrassing question. It would have been exceedingly difficult for me to have replied to these observations of the Secretary of State, without incurring the risk of giving farther cause of displeasure to his lordship, because any explanations I could offer, however well-intended, were likely to fall far short of his lordship's requisitions. The depositing in the archives of Van Diemen's Land of Lord Stanley's unmitigated denial and broad and flat contradiction of all my statements, seemed to me to meet in the fullest manner the reason alleged by his lordship for addressing his despatch to my successor, and to fulfil every object which he could reasonably desire*. Moreover the tone of his lordship's despatch was ill-

* Lord Stanley's intention was to leave on record in the same place where the charges were deposited, his "equally formal and public" refutation of them. His lordship's object has been fulfilled perhaps beyond his intention, The public in Van Diemen's Land were in profound ignorance of the contents of the four despatches and letters referred to by Lord Stanley, one-half of which were written after my retirement from the government, and did not necessarily form part of the archives of Van Diemen's Land. The same re-

calculated to remove or alleviate the unpleasant feelings which his lordship's previous conduct towards me had excited, and to have replied to it under the influence of irritation, and when I was still looking for the adjustment of differences and the compensation of injury, would have been as impolitic as unbecoming. Nevertheless I was glad of the opportunity afforded me a few days after, to give to Lord Stanley personally an explanation of one of the passages which had displeased him, and which on reperusal appeared to me capable perhaps of bearing an offensive construction which I had not intended*.

In pursuance of a subject which is likely to embarrass the thread of my narrative if not at once disposed of, I may add, that at a subsequent period, but before any result had arisen from the interview with which Lord Stanley honoured me, I learnt that his lordship had expressed his expectation that I should have answered the letter and despatch above alluded to. On obtaining this information I lost not a moment in addressing to Lord Stanley such apologetic explanations of any hasty or indiscreet expressions in my series of quoted despatches as were called for either by the personal explanation into which his lordship had condescended to enter with me on some minor points, or by his assurance that I had totally misunderstood his own habits and the course of proceeding invariably observed in his office. I assured his lordship that I had not the remotest intention in anything I had said to question his vigilant administration of his department, or his desire at all times to do impartial justice. As I had been also informed, to my great surprise, that his lordship's under-secretaries considered themselves included under the term subordinates, I hastened to assure his lordship that no such intention had existed in my mind, and

serve does not appear to have been observed respecting his lordship's reply. My communications from Van Diemen's Land lead me to believe that even its phraseology, on some points at least, is familiar to the public. This may not be an improper place to state, that up to this day my communications with Lord Stanley, whether verbal or written, have not been transmitted to the colony.

* The passage referred to, I explained by the practice of *précis*-writing; if the *précis*-writer be not absolutely indifferent to the issue of the case he deals with, or be not severely trained in the habit of subduing his own partialities, an unfair conclusion may be arrived at. Lord Stanley, by assuring me that he had examined all my despatches himself, thought fit to dispel an illusion to which my implicit faith in his lordship's justice and candour had helped in a great degree to make me cling.

expressed my regret that the term should have been considered capable of this extended signification *.

My letter bore date the 13th of August, and was sent on that day. It had not been received by Lord Stanley when he wrote one to me, bearing the same date, but which I did not receive until the 14th.

In the last paragraph of this letter, Lord Stanley expresses his dissatisfaction at my having left his despatch to Sir Eardley Wilmot of the 31st of January preceding, unanswered, and his opinion that I should either have adduced the evidence on which my charges were founded, or admit, that under irritated feelings, I had made them without sufficient consideration. My letter above mentioned, which Lord Stanley had not at the moment received, did not meet his lordship's requisitions on these points. It seemed to be expected from me that I should acknowledge that no influence had existed, and had been used against me, in Lord Stanley's office; no *ex parte* statement received or acted on there; that no improper transpiration of news had been traced to it; no slanderous statements listened to in that office, circulated there, and thence extensively disseminated. This was pressing me too far; the evidence of these facts was before me, and much of it was before Lord Stanley also. My charges were specific enough, and it rested with Lord Stanley to make such inquiries into his own office as would enable him to know where the fault lay. The correspondence on this subject terminated unsatisfactorily, but not till a period far beyond that when all hope of redress on my part from Lord Stanley, on the causes I had of complaint, had been peremptorily extinguished.

My interview with his lordship took place on the 18th of June. Of this interview I shall say in a few words that his lordship said little, and listened patiently. He assured me however that my recall was not connected with Mr. Montagu's suspension, but had been delayed a few months in order to disconnect the two events †. I assured his lordship that it was not of my recall at

* To Mr. Stephen, with whom I had had the honour of a personal acquaintance, and whose impression on this point was peculiarly painful to me, I addressed a private letter, which he kindly assured me was satisfactory.

† As Lord Stanley desired it to be understood that my recall had nothing to do with Mr. Montagu's suspension, it is to be regretted he had not resisted the pressure which apparently made him act as if the one were the necessary consequence of the other. The movements of the Colonial Office are better understood in Van Diemen's Land than his lordship supposes. It was well known that my post was considered vacant as soon as his lordship had pro-

the usual period, and still less at a period beyond even the usual one, that I should have thought of complaining, had it not been for the circumstances which preceded and attended it; neither was it his lordship's disapproval of a particular act of my government, of which he was the official judge, that I felt I had a right to arraign, but because no reasons whatever were given me for that disapproval; because Mr. Montagu's assertions had in every case been preferred to mine, and the grounds for such a judgement withheld from me; moreover, because the terms in which that judgement was conveyed could not but be exceedingly painful and injurious to me; yet being such, they had been given to Mr. Montagu, who had no right to them, without any shadow of consideration for me, and had been by him, as might have been expected, made public. I took the liberty of remarking to Lord Stanley, that I believed this act of giving to an inferior officer a transcript of the exact terms in which his superior was censured, was without a parallel in the annals of his office. Lord Stanley answered me nothing, except by an expression of some incredulity or surprise at finding his despatch had been published in an English newspaper. When I mentioned that the reference to Lady Franklin in equivocal terms in that despatch made the injury more poignant, and was proceeding to point out how its publication had given impunity to the attacks of the press, under corrupt influence, his lordship arrested me by expressing his extreme repugnance to the bringing the name of a lady into the discussion. It was not in my power to respect this scrupulous delicacy on his lordship's part, which does

nounced his decision on Mr. Montagu's case. It was so spoken of by members of Mr. Montagu's party in Van Diemen's Land,—the highest authority recognized at that time in the Colony for Downing-street information. If this be the case, the putting off to the latest moment the gazetting of the new governor and the official communication to me, whatever other advantage these delays may have possessed, could not have had that of widening the distance between the two events, viz. the non-confirmation of Mr. Montagu's suspension and my recall. The only apparent disconnection was this,—that the terms of my recall were not put into the same despatch as that containing the judgement of the Secretary of State on Mr. Montagu's suspension. It was well known that before my answer to that despatch could reach England, my successor was far advanced on his voyage to Van Diemen's Land. In fact, the interval between the issue of the despatch on Mr. Montagu's suspension in September 1842, and the embarkation of Sir Eardley Wilmot in March 1843, was scarcely more than sufficient under ordinary circumstances for the maturing of the arrangements necessary to the change. Nevertheless, as Lord Stanley has condescended to assure me that it was his intention and wish to disconnect the two events referred to, I am bound to accept and acknowledge his intended consideration.

not appear to have existed, if Mr. Montagu were correct in his assertion, when Mr. Montagu's calumnious statements respecting that lady were made to his lordship, and which seemed therefore somewhat unseasonable when the question was only of her justification; but this is a part of my communications to his lordship on which it becomes me perhaps to be silent.

On my remonstrance upon the injury done to my authority in the colony, by making the injurious observations of a colonial newspaper, which I had myself brought before his lordship's notice as the organ of Mr. Montagu's sentiments, the ground of calling upon me for an explanation of my conduct; and on my further remonstrance, that I had received no acknowledgement of the explanation thus called for and duly submitted, Lord Stanley replied, that he thought I had received an answer; and farther alleged, that it was necessary to be prepared with a reply to any questions which might be put to him in the House on such subjects. I refrained from remarking to his lordship, that probably the most rigid and minute investigators in that house into the conduct of public men would not think it necessary to drag before the eye of the British public the name of the governor's wife and her supposed palanquin-bearers, which formed the *gravamen* of the antipodean newspaper's charge; and that if a secretary of state for the colonies and his governors were to be prepared to answer all the tribe of colonial prints, they would have enough work upon their hands. It was clear to me that his lordship's attention could not have been *spontaneously* given to the consideration of this paltry subject.

With respect to that act of my government which Lord Stanley had not waited to have explained by myself, who was the only competent person to explain, but which he had condemned and reversed on the private representations of a subordinate officer, who was the person most interested in overturning it, his lordship admitted the fact, adding, that Mr. Forster's friends had come about him, and that he might perhaps have been himself the person to have communicated his decision to one of them before it was officially transmitted to me. The candour of this admission took from me all desire to reply.

As to my general report on the changes I had introduced in convict discipline, and of which the arrangement respecting Mr. Forster had been the only portion Lord Stanley had hitherto noticed, his lordship observed, that the despatches on that subject having crossed each other, he had been unable to make use of mine, but had transmitted instructions, that, where advisable or practicable, my suggestions should be attended to.

On that embarrassing subject which the revelations of Mr. Montagu's book had brought to light, and on the conduct of Mr. Montagu and his friends in the composition and circulation of that book, I did not expect Lord Stanley to say much, but he said less than I expected. I was suffered indeed to enter almost without interruption into a variety of details in illustration of this subject. It would have been difficult to have guessed whether his lordship knew but little and wished me to unburthen my mind for his information, or whether, having already heard much, he might not be seeking for the means of comparing parallel or conflicting statements; or rather, whether, as he had apparently given an unchecked hearing to Mr. Montagu's statements, when Mr. Montagu had nothing to gain by making them, because everything had been gained already, he might feel it but right to grant an equal degree of indulgence to me, whose only object was self-defence. However this might be, Lord Stanley refrained from expressing any sentiments on Mr. Montagu's conduct, yet he intimated to me that the case might be re-opened and undergo a revision. I left his lordship under the impression that I should hear again from him on this subject when he had given it due consideration, and that in the meantime I should at least be honoured by a letter expressing to me that cordial approbation of my government, the omission of which, in my letter of recall, I had considered equivalent to censure, and which his lordship had intimated to me might yet be supplied. I refrained from suggesting any mode or terms by which this acknowledgement might be effected, conceiving that it was more becoming in me to leave the adoption of these to Lord Stanley's justice and generosity.

That his lordship, even under the pressure of parliamentary labour, which at that time weighed on him, could not wholly forget the humble, perhaps, but undoubtedly just claims I had on his consideration, I was well aware, for they had been again at intervals submitted to his lordship from several quarters which could not fail to command his attention; yet week after week passed away without either summons or letter, and but for an occasional demand upon me for an explanation on points of expenditure from the Lords of the Treasury, which were transmitted to me in the ordinary course from the Colonial Office, the memory of the facts I related in that office, which I never afterwards approached, might be supposed to have passed away.

There was one circumstance however in my interview with Lord Stanley which appears to have left some traces on his lordship's mind: I had on that occasion placed in his lordship's hand the original document in Mr. Montagu's own handwriting, and bearing his signature, on which the expensive alterations in St. George's Church, Hobart Town, had been carried on without my knowledge *.

Lord Stanley was already in possession of the means by which that document had come into my possession, and of the judgement of the Executive Council upon it.

On the 15th of July I received from his lordship an account of the defence made by Mr. Montagu when called upon to reply to this charge, and which his lordship deemed satisfactory; his lordship farther informs me, that having disposed of this case in the manner communicated to me in No. 150, my subsequent despatches had not led him to perceive any material alteration in its features, though one of them, it must be remembered, No. 95 of the 19th of July 1843, had communicated the discovery of the lost document.

The unanimous opinion of the Executive Council appears to have had more weight with his lordship than my own unaided statements, and accordingly, his lordship proceeds to add, that he considers it due to me now to state that he concurs in the opinion of the Council, and that it appears to him that Mr. Montagu was in error in supposing that I was acquainted with and approved of the alteration in the plans of St. George's Church. At the same time his lordship sees no reason to attribute to Mr. Montagu any corrupt motives in the matter, and being able to conjecture in what way such an inaccuracy might take place, considers that no useful end would be attained by prolonging a discussion on the subject.

Lord Stanley miscalculated my deference to his judgement when he expected me to be satisfied with such a measure of justice as this. With no inclination to question his estimate of Mr. Montagu's motives, thus tenderly protected, I remonstrated against the position in which his lordship was willing to place

* See Appendix (G.) for the authority in question indorsed on a note addressed by Mr. Logan, one of the Churchwardens, to Mr. Montagu.

me, and which appeared to me to be that of a man relieved of a charge made against himself, instead of that of a person who had established by irrefragable evidence the charge he had brought against another. I pointed out to his lordship that in adopting the opinion of the Council, he had stopped short of its comprehensiveness, for that the Council had not only pronounced that *I* had *not* given the authority for the church, but that *Mr. Montagu had*. I humbly conceived that an explicit recognition of the latter fact was due to me, and the more so, if the statement were true which Mr. Montagu laboured to disseminate in the colony, that my charges on this subject had injured me more in Lord Stanley's mind than any of the others I had brought against him.

On the 3rd of August, nearly seven weeks after the interview which Lord Stanley had accorded me, I addressed a letter to his lordship, in which I took the liberty of respectfully reminding him that I was still anxiously awaiting the result of his consideration on the points I had personally and in a series of despatches submitted to him. This letter was accompanied by a separate paper containing a summary of the points alluded to, in order that his lordship might again be made fully aware of the grounds of my appeal. And in order that his lordship might be in no doubt as to how much I desired from him, or how little I should be satisfied with in reply to my representations, I ventured in my letter to submit to him the following requests:—

1st. I submitted how indispensable it was for me to be assured by his lordship of his belief, that in my suspension of Mr. Montagu I was actuated solely by a desire of the public good, and not by personal or private motives*.

2ndly. I requested an expression of Lord Stanley's opinion upon the conduct of Mr. Montagu in transmitting for circulation to the colony under my government, his recorded account of certain defamatory statements made by him in the Colonial Office, as well as upon the conduct of those officers of my late government who had aided in the circulation of the same†.

* This was necessary to meet the assertion made by Mr. Montagu and not repudiated by Lord Stanley, that his suspension was solely attributable to Lady Franklin's hatred of him and influence over me.

† It will be perceived that my request was limited to that portion of Mr. Montagu's conduct in which Lord Stanley had no part. Whatever might be the nature of my reflections upon Lord Stanley's condescension in learning from a subordinate officer, after he had decided upon his case, the opinions of that officer upon the conduct and capacity of the governor who had dismissed him, yet so long as no note of these conversations transpired beyond the walls

3rdly. I solicited an assurance of Lord Stanley's acceptance of my statement, that it was Mr. Montagu, and not myself, who gave the authority for certain building alterations in St. George's Church *.

4thly. I trusted that if the explanation I had been called upon to give of my conduct in granting certain rewards to meritorious convicts, which had been called in question on the authority of a local newspaper, appeared satisfactory to his lordship, I might be favoured with an acknowledgement to that effect.

And again, that if I was correct in thinking that Lord Stanley had expressed his favourable opinion of my views on Convict Discipline, as successfully worked during the last year of my government, and which had been reported in despatches that crossed his lordship's instructions on the same subject, I should not be refused the written expression of that sentiment†.

5thly. I solicited the written expression of Lord Stanley's assurance that my recall was unconnected with Mr. Montagu's suspension, and that the circumstances attending it were unintentional‡.

6thly. I reminded Lord Stanley of his personal assurance to me, that the omission of any expression of approbation in the despatch announcing my recall was not intended for censure, and expressed my conviction that if the anxious efforts I had made, worthily to keep the high trust which had been reposed in me during the usual period of a colonial government were appreciated by him, as they had expressly been by the great body of the colonists, this indispensable testimony would be supplied.

Lastly. I requested that a copy of any communication embodying these points, with which his lordship might be pleased

of the official chamber in which they took place, what passed on that occasion could only be considered as strictly confidential. But when a written and minute statement of these private communications was sent out to the colony itself for circulation, to the derogation of the governor's authority and character, then, a cognizable and even flagrant act of impropriety was committed, which I felt sure Lord Stanley could not have foreseen, and when called upon, could not but condemn.

* A reference to p. 107 will show that this request was still called for ; and even had Lord Stanley's letter to me on this subject been entirely satisfactory, it was a private document which I had no means of placing amongst the public records.

† Lord Stanley's favourable consideration of these two points was slightly intimated in his personal communication with me, but the expression of it could not of course be made use of by me until it was deliberately recorded.

‡ The assurance already given by Lord Stanley in the personal interview required only to be written.

to honour me, should be transmitted to the Lieutenant-Governor of Van Diemen's Land, with directions that it should be laid before the Legislative Council at their next setting.

For such a step, which was indispensable in order to place me in a proper position in the eyes of the colonists who had witnessed the attempted degradation of my government and character, I had already adduced to Lord Stanley the example of one of his lordship's predecessors, and I ventured to express my conviction that the act would be acceptable to the people of Van Diemen's Land, and would tend to strengthen their confidence in and attachment to Her Majesty's Government*.

In conclusion, I expressed my trust that Lord Stanley, in considering these requests in connexion with the various points on which I felt myself aggrieved, would perceive that the redress for which I looked to him was bounded by a perfect recollection of our relative positions, and by profound respect for his lordship's dignity and high office. His lordship would perceive that I had refrained from pressing my own claims at the expense of an officer whom he had seen fit to uphold, and whom I did not desire to injure; but in saying this, I could not avoid expressing my determination not to shrink from any exposure of the machinations which had been used to injure me, if the interests of my character should demand it; adding, that, exceedingly painful as such a course would be to me in the circumstances both private and professional in which I was placed, I had deliberately looked to it as my only remedy should every other fail me. I told Lord Stanley that I felt it to be my duty to say this, as the only proof I could give him of the depth of my sense of injury, and I besought his lordship rightly to appreciate my motive.

Being most anxious that Lord Stanley should not precipitate a reply which would have to me such important consequences, I requested that he would previously grant me another interview, or if it were equally agreeable to him, that he would permit me to fix upon one of my friends to wait on him in my place, in which case I would beg his lordship's reception of my much-esteemed friend Mr. Robert Brown, of the British Museum, a request which was immediately granted for a distant day.

I think it will be apparent from the account I have here given,

---

* Publicity on such reparation as the Secretary of State was enabled to afford me, could alone meet the injurious effects of the publicity of his lordship's despatch.

that I was not unmindful of Lord Stanley's position, and that if his lordship had had any doubt hitherto as to the nature of the redress which I expected from him, he must now be aware that it was restricted within limits which showed how anxious I was to save him from embarrassment, and to avoid even the appearance of asking him for an acknowledgement of error. His lordship's despatch could not be unpublished; his acceptance of Mr. Montagu's calumnies I could not even desire to convict him of; his restoration of Mr. Forster could not be undone. These and many other points on which I felt deeply aggrieved, I refrained altogether from even alluding to in my letter of requests, because the only reparation of which they were susceptible involved admissions which I did not expect, and acknowledgements which, to be of any value, should be graciously and spontaneously conceded; but with so much the more reason did I conceive that on the few points submitted I ought to obtain ample satisfaction. I gave to Mr. Brown, therefore, no other instructions previous to his waiting upon Lord Stanley in my behalf, than that he should, if necessary, impress upon his lordship the moderation of my requests, and the impossibility on my part of my resting satisfied with the disregard of any one of them.

Of the interview in question, which took place on the 12th of June, all that I shall permit myself to state, is, that it elicited from Lord Stanley an acknowledgement that Mr. Montagu had been permitted, both to his lordship and to Mr. Hope, to make those injurious representations respecting myself and Lady Franklin which are recorded in his 'book'; nay, that he had placed a memorandum to that effect in Lord Stanley's office.

In order that there might be no doubt of the identity or similarity of the statements made to Lord Stanley and Mr. Hope, with those recorded by Mr. Montagu in his book, Mr. Hope was requested to read, and did accordingly read in Lord Stanley's presence the letter of Mr. Young, as given in the Appendix, which contains a selection from, or, as another witness states, a portion only of the offensive and reprehensible matter dispersed throughout that section of the book.

Lord Stanley informed Mr. Brown that he would write to me in the course of two or three days; but in this instance the deed anticipated what the promise held forth, and the very next day, too soon even for his lordship's receipt of my instant acknowledgement of an observation made by him to Mr. Brown, that he had not received a reply to his despatch to Sir Eardley Wilmot*, the letter was written, within the compass of which I was to find all my indemnification for those months and years of trial and endurance which I have imperfectly described in the foregoing pages.

The letter of Lord Stanley of the 13th of August being intended I presume for such publicity as I thought proper to give it, as well as being the measure of reparation which his lordship has deemed sufficient for the case, I give verbatim with my comments; premising that for its full understanding, it is necessary to read the extracts from Mr. Montagu's letter to Mr. Stephen, which are referred to in it. They are given in Appendix (**K**).

" Sir, " Downing-street, 13th August, 1844.

" In compliance with your request, I yesterday saw Mr. Brown of the British Museum, in reference to the causes of complaint which you conceive yourself to have against the Colonial Office. I did not however gather from that gentleman anything which had not been already fully represented to me by yourself in person, and in the voluminous correspondence which you have from time to time transmitted. Adverting now to your letter and statement of the 3rd instant, I must beg to observe, that until I received it, I was not aware that you were in expectation of any farther communication from me†; nor do I indeed now know what is the 'immediate decision' to which you expect me to come‡.

" I regret to find that I have been unsuccessful in removing from your mind, by reiterated explanations §, the impression not only that you were recalled from your government as a mark of disapprobation, but that the course I adopted subsequently to my disapproval of your suspension of Mr. Montagu, and every step

---

* See p. 100–102.

† See p. 106 for the grounds of my expectation that I should receive some farther communication from Lord Stanley.

‡ The phrase had reference to the suspense in which I had so long been kept, as well as to the specific points then submitted to his lordship's judgement.

§ I am at a loss to account for his lordship's impression that he had given me " reiterated explanations ;" but if the term applies to his having said the same thing to me twice over, or even more often in the one interview I had with him, I am constrained to observe, that no repetition of his lordship's verbal explanation, however acceptable to me, could compensate for the absence of any tangible expression of it.

which I took was calculated to lower you in the eyes of the colonists, and to embarrass your government. I have in vain explained to you the very different motives by which I was actuated, and the accidental circumstances which produced some of the results of which you complain, and I certainly was both surprised and pained, to find all these circumstances again formally enumerated, in the statement which you have now transmitted to me*.

" I did not, and I do not think that the charges on which you suspended Mr. Montagu were sufficiently substantiated to justify that course of proceeding.

" I came to that conclusion on a careful perusal of the documents transmitted by yourself and none others†, and not (as you have repeatedly asserted, and without any evidence to justify the assertion, and notwithstanding the most formal contradictions,) upon ex-parte statements and private representations of Mr. Montagu or his friends‡.

" Nor are you correct in representing that I was called upon to decide, or did in any way decide upon the credibility of two parties§. I had to decide whether the charges which you

* Lord Stanley confuses the grounds of my complaint by blending deliberate measures with accidental circumstances, and under cover of this confusion, I am made to appear as obstinately refusing to accept the explanations which on a few points his lordship condescended to offer me. These points are enumerated in my letter of the 3rd of August.

† " *And none others.*" This is a startling assertion. Lord Stanley, in his despatch No. 150, gave me to understand that Mr. Montagu had answered all my charges, one after another, in the most satisfactory manner ; again, in the interview of the 18th of June, that he had judged the case entirely on Mr. Montagu's *written defence* (meaning, not on his verbal representations, which were then under discussion), portions of which *written defence* he transmitted to me in his letter of the 15th of July on the St. George's Church case.

‡ It would have been still more satisfactory had his lordship been able to assure me that no opportunities had been afforded to Mr. Montagu of making ex-parte statements and private representations either to his lordship himself, or to any of the officers of his department, prior to his lordship's decision. It must have been very difficult for Lord Stanley to extract the pure, impartial conclusions he desired to make on the documents before him, from the prejudices he had imbibed through other channels, and which gave their tone and colouring to every paragraph of the despatch at the head of this narrative. If Lord Stanley had wished me to infer that he did not accept or does not retain the impressions Mr. Montagu conveyed to him, why does he deny me the satisfaction of telling me so ? he could be at no loss for language to convey such a sentiment without committing himself with me.

§ Lord Stanley must at least admit, that in a matter of conflicting evidence, Mr. Montagu's statements were invariably preferred to mine ; with how much correctness of deduction has been proved in the St. George's Church case. It required nothing less than the production of an irresistible document written and signed by Mr. Montagu himself, *and even then not until I had a second*

I

brought against Mr. Montagu of motives were substantiated*, and whether his conduct had been such as to warrant his removal. My opinion was in the negative; but that opinion did not imply any disbelief of your integrity or honour; nor did I ever impute to you, that in removing him you were not actuated by a sense of public duty†. Having come to that decision, I was bound to communicate it to the accused party; and thinking that he had been unjustly removed, I might unquestionably have sent him back to his office.

" If I did not take that course, it was solely in deference to your feelings, with a view not to embarrass your government, or place you in a position in which you must have tendered your resignation‡. Perhaps I erred in this respect; but if I did so, it was, as I have said, from consideration for you, and from nothing else.

" From the same motives, and being desirous that your recall at the expiration of the usual term of colonial government might not have the appearance of being connected with my disapproval of Mr. Montagu's removal, I postponed sending you the usual letter for some months.

" I conclude this is a sufficient answer to the fifth request in your present letter. I had hoped that my previous personal declaration to that effect would have rendered unnecessary the

time and in person enforced that document upon his lordship's attention, to convict Mr. Montagu in his lordship's opinion of error.

See p. 107, where it is admitted that the document was unattended to when first mentioned.

* I brought against Mr. Montagu, not the charges of *motives*, but of *actions* and the failure of duty.

† I am not sure whether Lord Stanley has perceived the drift of my application to him on this point, and that an acknowledgement of his lordship's belief that I was actuated by a sense of public duty in my suspension of Mr. Montagu, and not by any personal or private motive, at once sweeps away all Mr. Montagu's charges on that head. (See note at p. 108.)

‡ Until I received this assurance personally from Lord Stanley, I had concluded that, though my specific charge against Mr. Montagu had failed, yet that his lordship had not felt himself justified in resisting the serious representation I made to him, that even were my own removal resolved upon, Mr. Montagu ought not to be restored to a colony where he had already lived too long (see p. 37). Unquestionably the publication of the despatch did as much to embarrass my government, as any measure from which his lordship in consideration to me refrained. But Lord Stanley may have some ground for dissatisfaction at my want of due perception of that consideration, for he is probably conscious of having behaved to me with greater courtesy than under the influence of Mr. Montagu's accepted statements he thought was required of him.

repetition of the statement, that the postponement was felt by you to be a greater injury than your immediate recall would have been*. You are already aware of the circumstances (the ship conveying the despatch being driven back by stress of weather) which prevented your receiving notice of your recall six weeks or two months before the arrival of your successor. I have expressed my regret at the accident, but the declaration which you have made, that it must have been known at the Colonial Office that the vessel which took out these particular despatches was a notoriously slow sailer, is, I may be permitted to add, only one instance of that unfortunate ingenuity with which you appear to convert the most trivial circumstances into studied slights†.

" You call upon me to express my opinion of Mr. Montagu's conduct in forwarding to Van Diemen's Land, and causing to be extensively circulated, a book containing ' defamatory statements' with regard to yourself. On receiving your complaint on this subject, I called on Mr. Montagu for an explanation. I send you extracts from a letter which I received from him in reply [see Appendix H.]. The memorandum referred to was sent to me. It is not necessary, nor would it be right that I should communicate it to you‡. It contained expressions purporting to have been used, and which very likely were used, by Mr. Montagu to Mr. Hope and myself. That they were not

---

* The reader who has gone through the preceding pages, and recollects the embarrassment to which my government was subjected in consequence of the publication of Lord Stanley's despatch, and other measures of the Colonial Office, will not wonder that I should have considered my immediate recall as a much less injury.

But the observation is not made in my letter of requests, and required no notice from Lord Stanley in this place.

† Having, in the interview of the 18th of June, acknowledged the hasty conclusion to which I had in one of my despatches given expression on this point, and having neither repeated nor alluded to it in any form whatever afterwards, I should have been spared I think this observation. (See p. 88.)

‡ It is admitted by Lord Stanley, that he communicated to Mr. Montagu for his defence all the complaints I had made against him, yet he refuses to put me in possession of the memorandum embodying Mr. Montagu's statements against me. The nature of those statements may perhaps appear to Lord Stanley a sufficient reason for this incongruous proceeding, and it is not perhaps to be wondered at that he should object to reveal to me what he did not object to give ear to. Hence the safety of Mr. Montagu's policy. Lord Stanley did not foresee that Mr. Montagu, encouraged by the immunity given him, and in the intoxication of success, would himself have the effrontery to make public the machinery by which he had effected it.

favourable to you, by whom he had just been suspended*, is undoubtedly true; but they were, I must say, much less ' defamatory†' than much which you have placed on record in the Colonial Office with regard to Mr. Montagu. That gentleman having expressed his regret at the imprudence which led to even the limited circulation of that memorandum in the colony‡, I

---

* Lord Stanley might have substituted for this observation "over whom he had just gained a triumph," for Mr. Montagu's complete exculpation and his promotion to the office of Secretary to the Government at the Cape were already communicated to him when he indulged in these vituperative descriptions of the Governor who had recommended him to office; and at a later period than this, after he had received from Lord Stanley the complimentary, and altogether unexpected gift of a copy of the despatch addressed to myself, Mr. Montagu acknowledged the favour by a "few final stabs," more deadly than any of the preceding ones. (See Appendix C.)
Mr. Montagu's gratitude to Lord Stanley seems to have invariably found an outlet for its expression in abuse of myself.

† Lord Stanley in his advocacy of Mr. Montagu appears to forget that what I have placed on record in the Colonial Office was subsequent, and in answer to Mr. Montagu's statements in the "book," was written solely in self-defence, and was not merely provoked, but made necessary by Mr. Montagu's unexampled proceedings. If Mr. Montagu's statements are to be compared with any of mine, they should be compared with those made in my despatches respecting his suspension, in which, in remembrance of former friendship, I told Lord Stanley that "I had Mr. Montagu's welfare still at heart," and endeavoured as far as was in my power to secure his future honourable employment in some other field of action, whilst I deprecated his return to Van Diemen's Land.
That I have since said worse things of Mr. Montagu than he has said of me, I may readily admit; how could it be otherwise? I characterized his conduct as such conduct deserves to be characterized by every honest and honourable man; and if my sentiments are placed on record in the Colonial Office, it is a matter over which I have no control, but which nevertheless appears to me both right and proper, since where the poison is deposited, there also should be the antidote. Does Lord Stanley imagine, that having been with my wife publicly defamed by Mr. Montagu in England and in the colony under my government, I should address to him a mere *private* remonstrance upon it, or wait for a personal interview? Nevertheless, whatever observations I had to make upon Mr. Montagu's conduct were confined to my strictly official and privileged correspondence with Lord Stanley, not embodied in memoranda for circulation in society in England, or written down in a book, as Mr. Montagu's statements were, for circulation in Van Diemen's Land. The circumstances I have pointed out stamp Mr. Montagu's statements with the character of defamations cognizable as such in any court of law, and take from mine every shadow of resemblance to them.

‡ "*Even the limited circulation.*" Lord Stanley has condescended to assure me that he has read every word of my despatches himself. Were it not for this assurance, I should have presumed to doubt whether his lordship could have read a single word of that part of my despatch No. 95, of the 19th July, 1843, or its Appendix, wherein I speak of the contents, and the *extensive circulation* of Mr. Montagu's book. As these matters are capable of proof, and as I did not make my assertions without calculating that such

have not thought it necessary to take any further steps; but it
may be satisfactory to you to receive the assurance of Mr. Montagu, that in transmitting to his friends his own vindication, he
had no desire to embarrass your government*.

" You will excuse me if I persevere in declining to discuss
the question which was unfortunately raised of the interference
or non-interference of Lady Franklin in the affairs of government. I have frequently expressed my regret that any lady's
name should be introduced into discussions of this kind, and I
think it quite unnecessary that I should express any opinion on
the subject †.

might be called for, nor indeed without adducing at the time, the names and
statements of some of the most respectable individuals in Van Diemen's Land
as my authorities, I cannot but express my surprise, both at his lordship's
apparent contempt for those respectable authorities, and at the reliance he
appears to place in my ability to accept a statement so entirely at variance
with my knowledge of facts.

* It would be impugning the discernment of my readers to make any
lengthened comment upon this paragraph. The wretched excuse of Mr. Montagu, which Lord Stanley is so willing to accept for himself; the anxious ex-
tenuation of Mr. Montagu's fault, glaring as it is; the expectation expressed,
(not in mockery, for Lord Stanley would surely not condescend to use it towards me,) that I should be satisfied with Mr. Montagu's gracious assurance,
made moreover to the Colonial Office, and not to me, that in all he had done,
he had no desire (to annoy me or*) to embarrass my government, all attest
more forcibly than any words of mine can express, the embarrassment in
which Lord Stanley is placed by having suffered himself to be mixed up with
Mr. Montagu in this question.

† Any one reading this passage in Lord Stanley's letter would inevitably
suppose that I had requested his lordship to pronounce an opinion upon Lady
Franklin's conduct, and not only so, but had pressed it upon him with more
warmth than was becoming. The reader has before him every one of the requests I made to Lord Stanley in the language in which they were made, and
will see that I am justified in asserting that his lordship cannot point out to
me the passage in that letter in which I make any such appeal, or even hint
at it. Lady Franklin's name was deliberately and carefully kept out of sight
in my letter of requests, not only in order to spare Lord Stanley the necessity
of touching upon a delicate and embarrassing subject, but because I hoped his
lordship's reply would be of such a nature as that I could make use of it to my
own benefit, and in a document thus intended for a certain measure of publicity, I could not desire the introduction of a lady's name.

I may farther observe, that however desirous I may have been to remove any
impression which Mr. Montagu may have produced on Lord Stanley's mind
to my wife's prejudice, I could by no means think of requesting his lordship
to pronounce an opinion upon a point which I humbly conceive did not come
within his cognizance, which I alone was competent to decide, and for which
at least I alone was responsible.

I refer the reader to page 36 for the reasons which made me feel it necessary to guard Lord Stanley against the use which I had every reason to be-

---

* See Mr. Montagu's statement in the Appendix H.

" I think I have already informed you that I am satisfied that Mr. Montagu, and not you, signed the authority for certain alterations in St. George's Church, and that in that respect your statement was more correct than his.

" The papers transmitted fully bear out your assertion*.

" I do not hesitate also to state, that the explanation sent by you on the 11th of May 1842, in reference to a charge made against you by a colonial newspaper, was deemed satisfactory; had it been otherwise, it would have been my duty to prosecute the inquiry; but seeing a statement of facts which it was very desirable that I should be able on your part to contradict or explain, I thought that I was only performing a duty to you and to myself in desiring to be furnished with that explanation †.

" With regard to Convict Discipline, you are aware that the subject being one of great interest and importance, and on which I had long been expecting a definite proposal from you, I availed myself of the presence in this country of Mr. Montagu and Mr. Plunkett, the Attorney-General of New South Wales, and of Mr. Bicheno's early departure, to mature, in concert with Sir James Graham, a scheme, founded in great measure upon past experience, which was transmitted to you in my despatches of the 25th of November 1842, Nos. 175 and 176, and the 12th of December 1842, No. 182 ‡.

lieve Mr. Montagu intended to make of Lady Franklin's name, and without which precaution I conceived that very false and injurious impressions might be produced on Lord Stanley's mind of which I should ever remain *in ignorance*; Lord Stanley pays no attention to this fact, but would endeavour to throw upon my own want of sense of propriety, the odium of introducing into a discussion of this kind the name of a lady, who, it is left to be inferred, might have remained unmolested but for my self-inflicted act. It is worthy of remark, that though Lord Stanley here prominently and gratuitously brings forward Lady Franklin's name in a letter intended for publicity, he has carefully abstained from alluding to it in the part where Mr. Montagu's book was under discussion.

* Lord Stanley had not given me the explicit acknowledgement to which I was entitled on this point. It was on this account that I was obliged to trouble his lordship with a renewed application for it.

† Lord Stanley will not condescend to grant at my request an acknowledgement, which I might have expected gratuitously from his justice and courtesy, without making the offensive observation, that if I had not escaped condemnation under the first accusation, he would certainly have carried the matter farther; and yet in the same spirit which dictated and guarded every line of my letter of the 3rd of August, I refrained from any allusion to certain facts and circumstances respecting this transaction, which, while they aggravated the indignity shown me, would have been embarrassing to Lord Stanley to deal with. (See pp. 105 and 109, compared with pp. 55—57.)

‡ Though the "definite proposal" from me expected by Lord Stanley, did

" These despatches were crossed by others from you, informing me of the measures which you had simultaneously taken and provisionally introduced, and on the receipt of them I was happy to find that in the main they coincided with my own views, and that it was therefore unnecessary to add anything to the instructions I had already sent. I do not think it necessary to discuss the appointments which you made, and of which I was not informed by you until some months after I had learnt them through private channels *.

" Lastly, I have to assure you that the absence of any expression of approbation in the customary letter of recall was not intended to be in any way ' equivalent to censure.' I do not doubt, that during your administration of the government of Van Diemen's Land, your best endeavours were applied to an honest and faithful discharge of your duties, and certainly nothing came under my notice which could in any degree derogate from your high character for honour and integrity.

not arrive in England until after his lordship's instructions on Convict Discipline had been despatched, yet the *announcement* of my proposal, (showing that the latter would be speedily on its way, and also that I attributed great importance to my timely notice of it being received as soon as possible, for which purpose I transmitted it *viâ* India,) must have been received about a month previously (see page 44). I am at a loss to conceive why the early departure of Mr. Bicheno, who however did not leave England until *after* the arrival of the above announcement, should have been supposed to affect the matter in any degree; the Office-bags of the Colonial Department destined for Van Diemen's Land being as a matter of course sent by every convict-ship which sails for the colony, and in default of such, by any merchant-ship which is convenient.

* Who, on reading this observation, would suppose that it was meant as an answer to my just complaint, that Lord Stanley had restored Mr. Forster to an office which I had deemed it necessary to abolish (that of Director of the Probation Department), upon the private and premature representations of that officer, without even waiting to hear my reasons for a measure which was connected with arrangements of vital public importance? Undoubtedly this treatment of the Lieut.-Governor by Lord Stanley admits now of neither discussion nor redress, and accordingly, had Lord Stanley condescended to read my letter of the 3rd of August in the same spirit in which it was written, he would have seen that I refrained altogether from touching upon, or even alluding to, the subject; but throughout Lord Stanley's letter, it seems as if his lordship regarded as one and the same, my statement of the points on which I felt myself aggrieved, and my letter of requests, in which I omitted some of the most important of those injuries, in order to relieve his lordship from the difficulty of considering them. It may be that, disdaining to take cognizance of this respectful forbearance on my part, Lord Stanley has purposely introduced the points I avoided, in order to show the absolute scorn with which he could afford to treat them, or the skill with which they could be eluded; even under this supposition however, there is one point which his lordship does not even approach, I mean the publication of his despatch No. 150.

" I shall, if you desire it, communicate this correspondence, which you must allow me to hope may now terminate, to Sir Eardley Wilmot; but I do not think it necessary to instruct him to lay it before the Legislative Council, who, it appears to me, have nothing to do with the matter of which it treats*.

*   *   *   *   *

" I have the honour, &c. &c.,

" *Sir John Franklin, &c. &c.*"   " STANLEY."

The amount of Lord Stanley's testimony to the manner in which for nearly seven years I conducted the arduous government entrusted to me is (unless I greatly err in my construction of it), " as far as I know of you, you seem to me to be an honest man and to have done your best." It had been represented to Lord Stanley, that the injurious imputations contained in his despatch No. 150 were calculated to injure even my professional character, since energy and decision must be at least as necessary on the quarter-deck as in the council-room. I have not pressed upon Lord Stanley the same consideration. However indifferent his lordship may have been to the import of his words, I believe that it was as far from his desire as it was beyond his power, to inflict on me this injury; and had it been possible for me to have any doubts as to the first of these points, his lordship's explicit declarations would have forbidden their continuance. But however valuable may be to me Lord Stanley's opinion of the " honour and integrity " of my personal character, or his estimation of my professional one, neither the one nor the other can compensate to me for the absence of those expressions of approbation and respect from Her Majesty's Government at the close of my administration, which an *adequate fulfilment* of duty (not merely an exertion of " *best endeavours*") should command. It was not perhaps to be expected that a boon, for which I ought not to have been forced to ask, should, when asked for, be grudgingly conceded, or partially withheld. It may be that Lord Stanley could not conscientiously do otherwise. In either

---

* The remaining paragraph of Lord Stanley's letter is omitted, as having reference to the question which I have summarily treated of in p. 103, where the express subject-matter of the paragraph is given. My reply to his lordship's observations there quoted, and which, though written with perfect respect and candour, did not go far enough to satisfy his lordship, had not been received by him when he wrote this letter, but had crossed it on the way.

case, my business is to prove, if I am able to do so, that it has been withheld undeservedly, and unjustly.

I shall certainly not add to my list of public or private wrongs the refusal of Lord Stanley to make public in the colony his letter of the 13th of August. There remained for me but one more step to take, and on the 30th of August I addressed to his lordship the following letter :

" My Lord,　　　" Herstmonceaux, Sussex, 30th August, 1844.

" I should have had the honour to acknowledge earlier your lordship's letter of the 13th inst., if I had not considered it right to wait for some time after your lordship's receipt of mine of the same date.

" It is with infinite pain that I am under the necessity of stating to your lordship, that the terms of your lordship's letter are inadequate to afford me the satisfaction I expected from you ; and I regret this the more, because your lordship, having partially conceded to me a few of the points I had the honour to lay before you, though in language little conciliatory to my feelings, would appear to have anticipated a different result.

" This may be a sufficient reply to the question your lordship has been pleased to refer to me, respecting the communication of a copy of your lordship's letter to Sir Eardley Wilmot. As far as my own wishes are concerned, I can have no desire that a copy of it should be forwarded to Sir Eardley Wilmot.

" It would have been satisfactory to me to have been permitted to point out to your lordship the grounds of my inability to accept your lordship's letter as a reasonable reparation for the injuries I have received, but your expressed desire that the correspondence should terminate forbids my doing so.

" It may not be superfluous for me in the meantime to state, that neither in Van Diemen's Land, where the injuries I have received in my government are best understood, nor in this country, where, as well as in the colony, the unprecedented act has been witnessed of the publication in the newspapers of a despatch condemnatory of a Governor who was still in the exercise of his functions, can your lordship's letter, either in its substance or its terms, produce an impression which can at all counteract the evil that has been inflicted.

" I have the honour, &c. &c.,

" John Franklin."

" *The Right Hon. Lord Stanley, &c. &c.*"

I here close a narrative which has extended to a length unfavourable, I fear, to its general effect, and possibly even to its clearness. Being well aware of the importance of precise and circumstantial statements, I have been led into a minuteness of detail which required very numerous as well as careful references and collations. By treating of events, for the sake of greater accuracy and fidelity in the course in which they occurred, some repetitions also have necessarily been made which might have been avoided, had a subject once begun been carried on unbroken to its close.

But however much my narrative may have suffered from the conditions I have thus imposed upon myself, I trust that it will not be found to have failed altogether in its purpose, which has been that of vindicating the character of my government on a point upon which it has been assailed, and of bringing the truth to light wherever I conceived that honour and duty imperatively required it at my hands.

It was possible, nay, even easy, for Lord Stanley to have removed the necessity of this step; for though the past could not be recalled, he had at least the means of counteraction in his hands. The measure of reparation I was prepared to accept from his lordship could not have compromised him, and did not necessarily disturb any existing arrangements. I neither asked of Lord Stanley to undo his acts nor to recall his words, yet, though I thus respected his lordship's position and feelings, he has had little consideration for mine. I believe it is impossible for any one to read Lord Stanley's letter without feeling that it is a document, which, if his lordship had deigned to place himself for a moment in my position, he could not have written. I shall refrain from the expression of my feelings on some portions of it, and I trust I shall not be convicted of a captious or uncandid spirit when I remark, that even some of its admissions derive as much value from the evident reluctance with which they are made as from their intrinsic importance. It would appear that what Lord Stanley could not withhold, without withholding a reply altogether, he determined to render unpalatable.

Lord Stanley must be well aware that he has written me a letter which I can make no use of for the just and honourable purpose I had in view, and it is Lord Stanley himself who has forced me to make a use of it which he probably did not contemplate, and which I have not adopted without infinite pain and repugnance.

His lordship's despatch at the head of this narrative, and his letter at the close of it, explain at a glance my excuses for the step I am taking, and must convince every one that no man who values the blessing of an unsullied reputation could refrain from offering a counteraction of them, unless he laboured under some feeling of self-condemnation, or were withheld by a sense of incapacity or weakness.

And if there are any of my friends who conceive that I might afford to pass by the unmerited treatment I have received at the Colonial Office, because it is not the department in which my professional life has been passed and to which my affections and sympathies most closely cling, to them I must remark, that even in the point of view they suggest, I cannot forget that an eventful portion of my earlier years was spent in the career of discovery under its auspices.

But I may say more than this; for when I entered the service of Her Majesty, in the Department of her Colonies, I placed my honour in that service as thoroughly and as faithfully as in any other; and though Lord Stanley has not comprehended the spirit of my devotion to the public service, nor the loyalty of a heart as true to its allegiance in this as in any other field of duty, I owe it to myself to show that I know of no distinction in the trusts with which I am honoured, and have not been less solicitous to merit the approbation of my sovereign in the department of her Colonial government than in that of her Naval service.

As for the act which has led to so long a train of consequences,—I mean the removal of a high public officer from a place which I considered that he had justly forfeited, and in which his continuance appeared to me detrimental to the public interest,—it is one which I shall ever look back upon as justified by every principle of good government, and which, though it has entailed upon me evils which it ought not to have entailed, I trust I should not shrink from doing again, were the past once more in my power and the future known to me as the present is.

It was my intention to have made a few observations on the present state and the prospects of Van Diemen's Land under the operation of the existing system of unlimited and uncounteracted Convict Transportation; but this discussion, which involves many other auxiliary considerations, would lead me too far, and under the pressure of duties more imperative and now more immediately belonging to me, I have thrown aside my notes upon the subject, happy in the belief that the colonists of Van Diemen's Land will have no doubt of the interest I take in a matter of such vital importance to them as well as to the British Government, and still happier in the conviction that the deliberate and anxious efforts of the Secretary of State for the Colonies are given to remedial measures.

The cure of the evil, in its very nature rapidly progressive, cannot be applied with the celerity which the case demands, and no one who has the welfare of Van Diemen's Land at heart, but will desire that hope as well as patience will revisit her mansions and her homesteads, and retain her unsettled and anxious colonists within the sphere of their accustomed labours, sympathies and duties.

POSTSCRIPT.

My latest communications from Van Diemen's Land include some documents so highly illustrative of the conduct of Mr. Montagu, and of the character of that policy by which he has effected his objects, that I deem it right to publish them entire, leaving to the discernment of the reader to make such observations as they naturally suggest, and subjoining a few notes of my own only where they appear to me absolutely called for.

I am informed that Dr. Turnbull had been advised to publish the correspondence in Van Diemen's Land, Mr. Montagu having in this, as in other instances, sent copies of his own statements there for circulation.

The following article from the ' Hobart Town Advertiser' of the 25th October 1844, proves the notoriety of the correspondence :—

" We have the gratification to announce to the public, that Lord Stanley has expressed to Captain Montagu his entire satisfaction in regard to the ' Book.' Lord Stanley did not come to this determination until he had carefully perused it, and we repeat he *then* expressed his entire satisfaction at the whole of Captain Montagu's conduct in respect thereto."—*Murray's* ' *Review.*'

" We fear we must dispel this illusion. In this, as in the affair of *the book* itself, the Editor of the Review has not been taken into the confidence of his *protégé.* So far from Lord Stanley having expressed his approbation of Captain Montagu's conduct, that gentleman has himself most serious misgivings on the subject. Perhaps the Editor of the Review is not aware that there is at this instant a correspondence in the colony, in which that gentleman has requested that a memorandum of events might be verified which contradicts some of the strongest statements against him ; that he has accompanied it with a letter, in which he alludes ' to the tenacity of his own memory, and the defect of that faculty in another, and requests that the *facts* related some time since, which tell very much indeed against him, may be reviewed and *remembered* as he relates them ; '—that his relation has, however, met with a flat contradiction, and that the correspondence bears the strongest internal evidence that it has been entered into in consequence of Lord Stanley requiring that some discrepancies in Sir J. Franklin and Mr. Montagu's statements may be reconciled, which, as they are direct contradictories, is of course an impossibility.

" We said all along, that in the affair of the ' Book,' Captain Montagu had forgotten his habitual caution in the triumph of momentary success. His correspondence shows that he has now discovered his error, that he would repair it, if possible ; but the answer he has received, will, no doubt, show him, that truth is in the end all-powerful ; and that there requires to make up a case, not merely a very good memory in the concoctor, but a very pliant one in the witnesses. In the latter part, Mr. Montagu has not been quite so successful as he could wish.

" We are not just at present at liberty to make further use of this correspondence, but it is by no means unlikely that it may be published ; and then Mr. Montagu will, under his own hand, have shown that the character, long since attributed to him, was neither a false one in his youth, nor abandoned in his manhood."—*Hobart Town Advertiser.*

Cape of Good Hope, 30th April, 1844.

My dear Turnbull,—In December last I received letters from Van Diemen's Land, dated in May 1843, informing me that Sir John Franklin had called upon you to make him an official statement in writing of what had occurred in conversation between you and me in January 1842, upon the occasion of my sending to Lady Franklin to negociate a reconciliation between Sir John Franklin and myself, a few days after he had suspended me from the office of Colonial Secretary of Van Diemen's Land.

My letters inform me that you intend sending me a copy of your statement to Sir John Franklin, but it has not yet arrived, which I much regret, as I should have preferred observing upon it before giving you my own recollection on the subject. Not having heard from you, I have prepared a memorandum upon it, and transmit it herewith, rather than permit any further delay.

I understand you have expressed the opinion that I was not justified, after that conversation, in introducing Lady Franklin's name at all in my defence to Lord Stanley, and that you are of opinion that I so pledged myself upon the occasion referred to*.

I am quite positive I never did make any such pledge.

To have made it would have been an act of *felo-de-se*, as my whole case turned upon the fact of Lady Franklin's improper interference in the business of the Government, which, because I noticed it to Sir John Franklin, led to his suspending me from office. Unless I could have

---

* Dr. Turnbull had expressed *no such opinion*. (See Dr. Turnbull's reply, which is given in the sequel.)

proved, as I did, that Sir John Franklin's proceedings against me, which terminated in my suspension, occurred in consequence of my having mentioned Lady Franklin's name to him, I should have been shut out from the means of showing the motives which induced him to take that step*. I proved that up to that day the most unlimited confidence subsisted between Sir John Franklin and me†; and how I was to have shown that that confidence and harmony ceased, without introducing Lady Franklin's name, I know not. To have made a promise not to mention her name at all, would have been tantamount to a declaration of justification of Sir John Franklin, because it would have deprived me of the means of exposing the only and true reason of his conduct towards me‡.

I fully admit that I pledged myself to you not to repeat to any one the conversation which passed between us upon the occasion referred to herein, for the reason you will find inserted in the accompanying memorandum. That pledge I have religiously adhered to, and I never mentioned it even to Mrs. Montagu until December last, when I heard that you felt it expedient to repeat it, first to the elders of your church, and afterwards to Sir John Franklin.

But I think I can show you from your own acts, that you have quite forgotten the facts of the case, and that you yourself could not at the

---

* Mr. Montagu here, with characteristic and most politic effrontery, avows the one leading principle of his plan of defence, which he carried through without compunction to the end.

† Admitting this to be true, that the most unlimited harmony existed between us up to a certain day, when he mentioned Lady Franklin's name, this does not prove what Mr. Montagu asserts. On the same day that he mentioned Lady Franklin's name, and *before* he had mentioned it, Mr. Montagu threatened me with his withdrawal of his usual co-operation, &c., and *from* that day he kept his word.

Even as respects the use of Lady Franklin's name, he committed a gross offence in so doing; but a greater when I offered him the proof that *all* his suppositions and statements were entirely opposed to facts, and he refrained from retracting what he had said, or acknowledging his mistake. Such behaviour might well excite *my* displeasure without involving Lady Franklin in the subsequent series of events. But though Mr. Montagu's assertion of the unlimited harmony and confidence which subsisted between us up to that day does not prove what he would wish in this instance, it *does* prove that his representations of Lady Franklin's disturbing and habitual interference in the affairs of government is without foundation.

‡ Mr. Montagu here avows the desperate necessity which drove him to the defence he employed.

time alluded to, have supposed that I ever pledged myself not to mention Lady Franklin's name after that interview.

In the first place, you must remember that the conversation occurred on the 28th of January*, and that I remained in Van Diemen's Land until the 10th of February. During that interval there was scarcely a day that I had not several interviews with you, and at most, if not all, other persons were present.

Our conversations were naturally upon my case, and as the prominent point upon my mind and upon the minds of those I have alluded to, was respecting Lady Franklin's interference in Dr. Coverdale's case, and her subsequent conduct, and of the facility I should have from the evidence I had in my possession, of showing that my suspension was clearly to be ascribed to her feelings against me, it must have been evident to you at that time, that I was under no pledge not to mention her name in my defence, as I repeatedly and openly, as was well known to everyone I conversed with in Van Diemen's Land, stated that I meant to impute the blame to her, as having been the cause of my suspension. I could mention in detail several such conversations, but I think it unnecessary ; I will however mention one other circumstance, which, perhaps, will convince you that my recollection of the conversation is right and yours is wrong.

You may perhaps remember that the Rev. Mr. Aislabie wrote to me on the 7th of February to inform me, that with the private petition which was got up at Richmond to restore Dr. Coverdale, Lady Franklin had not anything to do, and it was not got up during her stay in that district (see page 29).

That letter I received on the 8th of February, and replied to it on the same day.

In my reply I stated, " that I, as well as others, had read in Lady Franklin's handwriting, that she did suggest to Mrs. Parsons the private petition in Dr. Coverdale's case†, and you are aware that a private

---

* The conversation in which Dr. Turnbull explained to Lady Franklin Mr. Montagu's wishes, and reported to him the result, took place *on the 27th of January*.

† When in the Richmond district, at the house of Mr. and Mrs. Parsons, Mrs. Parsons told Lady Franklin that it had been a question in the district whether the respectable inhabitants should not make a public representation to the Lieutenant-Governor of their desire that Dr. Coverdale should be reinstated,—Lady Franklin replied to the effect, that she saw strong objections to such a course, and thought individual, private and personal representation might be preferable. This private conversation, related in a letter of Lady Franklin's to me, and shown by me to Mr. Montagu, is the handwriting of Lady Franklin here referred

petition was subsequently adopted, and succeeded." Before sending
that letter I consulted with you, Mr. Forster and Mr. Charles Arthur,
upon it. We assembled in Mr. Forster's office, when all three advised
me to send it*, which I did, and Mr. C. Arthur then made a copy of it
on the back of Mr. Aislabie's letter, which original letter and copy are
now deposited in the Colonial Office in Downing-street. I then had
another copy of my letter to Mr. Aislabie made, as well as of his to me,
and sent them, under the same advice, on the same day to Sir John
Franklin, for his information.

Now surely if I had been under the pledge not to mention Lady
Franklin's name again, you would not have advised such a letter to
Mr. Aislabie; for you cannot have forgotten that all four of the persons
present agreed that such a statement respecting Lady Franklin's interference, transmitted as it was to Sir John Franklin himself, furnished a
most important link for the line of defence which all three of you knew
I intended to pursue before Lord Stanley on my arrival in England.

---

to. The letter of the Rev. Mr. Aislabie to Mr. Montagu, received by
Mr. Montagu before he left Van Diemen's Land (this letter is subjoined)
will show that this conversation had nothing whatsoever to do with the
petition which was subsequently presented from the district, and that
Mr. Montagu knew that it had not, by direct information from the
person who himself wrote the petition and procured the signatures.
Mr. Aislabie's statement to Mr. Montagu was direct and unequivocal,
that " it is untrue that the petition was got up during Lady Franklin's
stay in the district, and equally untrue that Lady Franklin had anything to do with it; or that he (Mr. Aislabie), with whom the letter
originated, took his idea from any other person." Mr. Montagu says
that he sent this letter to Lord Stanley; the reader will not be surprised
that I sent it also (see pp. 139, 140).

* Dr. Turnbull has passed this observation without notice. It may
be one of those points not specified, in which he says his recollection
differs from Mr. Montagu's; and Dr. Turnbull might well feel diffident
in bringing forward his own recollections when the evidence of three
persons would appear to be forthcoming against him. But however
this may be, I have a memorandum of an interview with Dr. Turnbull
on the 14th March 1842, in which he told me he had not seen Mr.
Aislabie's letter, and knew nothing of it but what the ' Van Diemen's
Land Chronicle ' had said ; he also told me that he had a perfect recollection of Lady Franklin's letter to me (the same as that referred to by
Mr. Montagu), in which she denies having recommended the petition
for Dr. Coverdale. Dr. Turnbull added, that he had read this in her
own handwriting.

ĸ

In addition to what I have stated respecting your own acts, I will now show you from Lady Franklin's acts that she never could have understood that I had pledged myself not to mention her name after my conversation with you of the 28th of January.

In the first place you must of course admit, that if I was pledged as you have stated, Lady Franklin thought she was equally pledged to the same effect; otherwise to require the fulfilment of such a pledge from one party only would have been an absurdity. That she did not consider herself pledged, is evident from the fact that one of Sir John Franklin's charges against me was that I had made an improper use of her name, and he transmitted to the Secretary of State a copy of the correspondence she had had with me * in the previous October respecting her interference in the Coverdale case. Now if we were mutually pledged that her name was not to be mentioned, why was this charge made, and the correspondence transmitted to Lord Stanley, if I had undertaken not to mention Lady Franklin's name at all?

I cannot suppose Lady Franklin would thus act against me under the belief that she could do so with impunity, because I was silenced by the pledge alleged. I hope I have said enough to convince you of your error, for error I am sure it is, from my knowledge of your character, and from my conviction that you would not say anything you did not believe to be true.

I have often heard you lament your deficient memory, and I have as often heard you express yourself in strong terms of the retentiveness of mine. I trust what I have now stated will produce a similar effect.

It has given me great pleasure to hear from Van Diemen's Land of the well-being of Mrs. Turnbull and your family, and I was very glad to find, after you lost the situation of Acting Treasurer, that Sir John Franklin augmented your income from £500 to £900 a-year, by allow-

---

* This is a mis-statement, but it is of little importance. The correspondence referred to I transmitted in February 1842 to Mr. Stephen, Under-Secretary of State, with a letter, in which I informed him of the application which Mr. Montagu had made to Lady Franklin for her intercession in his behalf.

The private nature of these documents, and the desire I felt not unnecessarily to reveal Mr. Montagu's unsuccessful application for restoration to office, induced me to request of Mr. Stephen that he would not make any use of these communications unless the protection of Lady Franklin should require it. My despatch, No. 3, 8th Feb. 1842, shows that in the same spirit I carefully guarded against Mr. Montagu's apologetic letter of the 31st of January 1842, being regarded, as it really was, as an application for restoration to office.

ing you to hold two or three appointments in addition to your own of Clerk of the Council. I hope, for your sake, that Sir Eardley Wilmot will not disturb the arrangement, though I should be afraid you would not be permitted to enjoy it very long*.

Believe me,

My dear Turnbull,

Yours very sincerely,

JOHN MONTAGU.

Memorandum.

Cape of Good Hope, 30th April, 1844.

On the 25th of January 1842, Sir John Franklin wrote and informed me that he should suspend me from office, and required me to name a day for delivering it over to my successor.

On the 27th of January, I wrote the letter numbered 1, to Sir J. Franklin.

During the evening of that day†, Dr. Turnbull called upon me and stated that he had just left Lady Franklin, who had expressed to him her great concern at the rupture between Sir John Franklin and me,—that he was sure she was quite sincere in her expressions of regard for me, and in her opinion of my value as a public officer, that he was sure she would willingly do anything in her power to bring about a reconciliation, but he distinctly informed me that he had made all this known to me without her knowledge, and that he was not au·thorized by her to make any communication whatever to me‡.

I told him I did not believe a word she had said, that I knew perfectly well she had directed every move Sir John had made against me, in consequence of my bringing her gross interference in Dr. Coverdale's

---

* The facts are grossly mis-stated, but it was expedient to convict me of committing, and Dr. Turnbull of accepting bribery.

† Mr. Montagu has omitted to state that on the *morning* of that day (27th) he sent Dr. Turnbull to Lady Franklin to open the business of mediation which he wished Dr. Turnbull to undertake for him; he is desirous of making it appear that this movement originated in Lady Franklin and not in himself, and puts off the result of it till the next day (28th), when Dr. Turnbull had no interview at all with Lady Franklin.

‡ As the conversation here introduced did not take place, it is unnecessary to make any observations upon it.

K 2

case under Sir John's notice—that I cared not for her sympathy, and needed not her mediation—we separated.

The next morning (28th of January) I sent for Dr. Turnbull, and told him I had further reflected on the previous evening's conversation. I said, I have not changed my opinion of Lady Franklin, and felt no doubt, from my own knowledge of her character, that she had an object in view which I do not at present discover, and I added, "Timeo Danaos;" but to this I superadded, that I considered I was bound to suppress my feelings in a matter of this kind, in order that I might be enabled to show my relations and friends that I had left nothing undone, consistently with the character and conduct of a gentleman, to avert the infliction of a suspension; for although I felt not the smallest particle of doubt that the result would be the reversal of Sir John Franklin's proceedings, yet under any circumstances the pecuniary loss must be very serious, in addition to the inconvenience and danger to Mrs. Montagu, whose delicate health with an infant but a few months old to nurse rendered the voyage painful and hazardous.

Under these circumstances I requested him to wait upon Lady Franklin, and inform her I was anxious for a reconciliation, and to request her to believe my most solemn assurance that I never intended any disrespect to Sir John Franklin, and hoped she would satisfy him thereon.

In about one hour Dr. Turnbull returned, and said Lady Franklin was much pleased at the message, and he saw a prospect of a reconciliation. He then produced my letter (No. 1.), which I had written the previous day to Sir John, and which he said Lady Franklin had given him* with a request that I would alter it in certain respects, so as to

---

* Lady Franklin did not give any letter to Dr. Turnbull; but she is made by Mr. Montagu throughout to originate every step in the affair.

The drift of Mr. Montagu's statement respecting the letter is this,— that I received a letter from Mr. Montagu, which through Lady Franklin and Dr. Turnbull was returned to him, and subsequently replaced by one altered from that which I originally received, though bearing the same date.

The facts are, that on the 28th I received Mr. Montagu's letter of the 27th; the original in my own possession is endorsed to that effect by myself. Mr. Montagu never directly or indirectly received any request to alter that letter after I had received it. I never received any letter but one of that date, and the one I possess neither replaced, nor was replaced by any other.

Mr. Montagu gives to his application to Lady Franklin a date which alone renders this transaction possible.

The point of this date is an important one, and Mr. Montagu, in his

make it more acceptable to Sir John Franklin. As there was nothing objectionable in the alterations proposed, I wrote the letter (No. 2.) while Dr. Turnbull remained with me, and sent it by him to Lady Franklin. I gave it the same date (27th January) as the letter it displaced. About three hours afterwards Dr. Turnbull came back to me. He said he had been with Lady Franklin during the whole interval; he seemed agitated, spoke as confidently as ever of Lady Franklin's sincerity for a reconciliation, and expressed his own hope that it would be brought about. He said she would effect it upon two conditions *, but that before telling me what they were, I was required to pledge myself not to mention to any one the conversations which passed, through him in this negotiation †, in the event of the reconciliation not taking place, and that Lady Franklin and Dr. Turnbull would pledge themselves in like manner. I consented. Dr. Turnbull said the conditions are, that I should advise Sir John Franklin in the Executive Council to build the college at New Norfolk and the bridge at Bridgwater, and that I would conduct the public business just as I did before the ' Coverdale ' affair occurred.

I replied, as respects the public business, I will conduct it in any way Sir John Franklin pleases; I have no feeling upon that subject, and

---

letter to Dr. Turnbull, says, " in the first place you must remember that the conversation occurred on the 28th of January. It will be obvious that had the right date (the 27th) been given by Mr. Montagu I could not have been made to have received a letter, the draft of which was shown to Lady Franklin late on that day, and which bears my own attestation of being sent to me on the 28th.

Dr. Turnbull, at the interview referred to, showed Lady Franklin a draft of a letter of apology from Mr. Montagu to myself; having read it, she remarked that she thought it was not the sort of letter which would be likely to remove my displeasure; that to have that effect a letter should, above all things, be honest and candid, have no mystification, and have some little warmth and feeling in it ; such a letter as the one Dr. Turnbull showed was not likely to do any good at all. It was no doubt this letter to which Mr. Montagu refers.

* A statement positively and distinctly contradicted both by Lady Franklin and by Dr. Turnbull. See in his letter to Mr. Montagu, his indignant comment on the observation.

† Mr. Montagu seems to have a distinct recollection of some pledge or other, but forgot that it was himself who exacted a pledge, and not Dr. Turnbull. The pledge Mr. Montagu exacted, was that of concealment of his application to Lady Franklin. He informed Dr. Turnbull that he did not intend to mention it even to Mr. Forster (his bosom friend and confidant).

will cheerfully obey any instructions he thinks proper to give me on that head. I added, the only difference since the " Coverdale " affair consists in this—previously I wrote my opinion upon the conduct of public officers and others upon the papers as they passed through my office on their way to the Governor, and of course before he had seen them; afterwards, with his express permission, I forwarded papers of that kind to him without such opinions; nor did I offer them subsequently, unless specially required to do so.

This constituted the whole difference. I added, I did not know, until I then learnt it through Lady Franklin and Dr. Turnbull, that Sir John required any change in that respect; I said, however, I would make it willingly*.

As respected the bridge at Bridgwater, I said to Dr. Turnbull, " You know as well as I do, that I have invariably advised the building of that bridge in the Executive Council, and so Lady Franklin can learn by consulting the Minute Book†." The opposition to that bridge had been made by other Members of Council and not by me. I could therefore have no difficulty in consenting to that part of the first condition.

But as respected the other part of the first condition, viz. to advise building the college at New Norfolk, I expressed my regret that Dr. Turnbull, who knew as well as I did all that had passed between Sir John Franklin and myself upon that subject, should have been the bearer of such a condition to me. He knew how sorely I had felt the proposition Lady Franklin had made to me the previous September (which I repeated to him and one or two other persons at the time), to prevail upon me to violate my oath of office as a Member of the Executive Council and Colonial Secretary, and to aid her endeavours to get that building erected ‡.

---

* All mis-stated. Lady Franklin thinks she may have remarked to Dr. Turnbull, that the way in which Mr. Montagu transacted business displeased me, but the exacting a condition was out of the question, and I need hardly add is positively denied by her.

† An insinuation of the same character as the others. The Minute Book of the Council was not open to Lady Franklin, as this remark implies. It was kept in my office, and Lady Franklin did not go there to consult the Minute Book or for any other purpose.

But Mr. Montagu reasons quite correctly about the Bridgwater bridge. It was known to be Mr. Montagu's hobby. The newspaper reports of the proceedings in the Legislative Council might have afforded Lady Franklin the amplest evidence that it was not necessary to stipulate for the bridge at Bridgwater.

‡ Mr. Montagu was opposed to the site of the college being at New

I told Dr. Turnbull, that neither the dread of any consequences, nor the offer of any earthly inducement could prevail upon me to accede to that part of the first condition, and if upon that point Lady Franklin remained firm, I should be equally so. He left me, and on the following morning he told me that Lady Franklin would not depart from that condition, and that my suspension must take place *.

The paper No. 3 gives the particulars of the New Norfolk College affair I have herein referred to.

JOHN MONTAGU.

Hobart Town, September 11, 1844.

SIR,—I have received and perused your letter of the 30th of April last, together with the Memorandum of the same date by which it is accompanied, and I shall now observe upon several of the points to which you advert.

1st. The information which you had received respecting my intention of sending you a copy of my statement is quite correct. I had indeed in July last prepared a copy for you, but at the request of the Lieut.-Governor (Sir John Franklin), who stated to me that by forwarding it then I should do him an act of injustice, I reluctantly altered that intention †.

2ndly. I do not remember ever to have expressed the opinion that

---

Norfolk, and in favour of a site near Hobart Town, on or adjoining Mr. Swanston's property at New Town. About a year before the conversation referred to by Mr. Montagu took place, I had deliberately fixed on the site at New Norfolk—had laid the first stone of the college in the presence of all the principal government officers, and a religious service had been performed on the spot. It was not likely that I should change it. The conversation to which Mr. Montagu refers took place at my own house at dinner. Lady Franklin, in a conversation which was carried on with perfect good humour on both sides, endeavoured to persuade Mr. Montagu that the site I had fixed on in the country was preferable to a site in or near the town, and tried to engage his interest in forwarding my efforts to get it erected. This Mr. Montagu calls "asking him to violate his oath of office."

* It is scarcely necessary to observe that it never entered into the mind of Lady Franklin to make, nor into that of Dr. Turnbull to propose, any conditions whatever. See Dr. Turnbull's flat contradiction of this statement of Mr. Montagu in Dr. Turnbull's subjoined letter.

† I objected to Dr. Turnbull's sending a copy of his statement, because I considered that Mr. Montagu should be left to his own unassisted recollection ! That I was right in this judgment, I think Mr. Montagu's letter and memorandum sufficiently prove.

you were not justified in introducing Lady Franklin's name at all, and I am quite certain that you never gave me any pledge not to do so.

The only pledge to which my recollection extends was one required by yourself, namely that the negotiation in which I had been engaged on your behalf should not be revealed, a pledge which so far as I am concerned was kept most faithfully until after the affair had transpired through another channel, and been denied in my own presence in a communication I had with Mr. Forster and Mr. Swanston, and until after I had learned that in the "Book" you had yourself stated that in the hearing of the Secretary of State you had imputed to her ladyship in terms of the most cruel reproach the having procured your removal from office.

Even then my first determination went no further than to reveal the negotiation to Mr. Forster, who was much astonished at what I told him, and requested me to inform Lady Franklin that up to that moment he had been in perfect ignorance of any such application having been made to her ladyship. But on the morning after I had done so, namely, on the 11th of May, I received a letter from Sir John Franklin, which led to my making the same communication to others, and which commenced as follows :—

"My dear Dr. Turnbull,—Nothing less urgent than the immediate contradiction of falsehood concerning a much-injured lady, would have caused me to intrude upon the solemn preparation which I am aware you are making, previous to the reception of the Holy Sacrament; but my dear wife having last evening made known to me, with your permission, the substance of your late communication to Mr. Forster, I feel that it would be a dereliction of the sacred and affectionate tie which unites us if I were to lose any time in conveying to you my sacred and solemn conviction that it is incumbent upon you personally to make a similar communication to Sir John Pedder and Mr. Swanston to that you have made to Mr. Forster."

Thus appealed to on a point as to which I had been undecided, I at once proceeded to the Derwent Bank and the Court House, but neither Sir John Pedder nor Mr. Swanston was in his office. I then called at Government House, and saw the Private Secretary, told him what I had done, and that I would endeavour to see them after the morning service.

I then went to church, and after the service had ended, I entered the vestry, where I found the Rev. Mr. Lillie of St. Andrews, the Rev. Mr. Bell of St. John's, Mr. Walker and Mr. Gunn. I at once told these gentlemen what had happened, and what I had been doing. I also read to them Sir John's letter, when they were all of opinion that I had no alternative but to protect Lady Franklin as I had been so solemnly required to do.

I need scarcely add that I again immediately went in search of Sir

John Pedder and Mr. Swanston. Such was the manner in which the different incidents occurred, and not as you have been erroneously informed. I may add, that two days afterwards, namely, on the 13th of May, Sir John Franklin called upon me in writing for a statement of the particulars, which however I did not furnish until the 3rd of June.

As I am clearly of opinion that you were not pledged not to mention to the Secretary of State Lady Franklin's name in connection with any facts really necessary to your defence, provided of course you did so in a manner not inconsistent with the position in which you had placed yourself with regard to her ladyship, it does not appear to be requisite that I should follow you through the arguments used by you to disprove the existence of any such pledge.

It may be right that I should mention that my recollection varies from yours in some particulars, but that I remember you appeared throughout occasionally to suspect the sincerity with which Lady Franklin had acted towards you, for at the very last interview which we had together, you asked me whether I thought she had been sincere ; and on the very last day of the mediation, when considering the terms of the letter to be addressed to Sir J. Franklin, which according to my recollection was not sent until the next day, you observed in effect, that Lady Franklin had acted ungenerously towards you in suggesting as necessary a retraction in writing of the obnoxious passage in your letter of the 17th of January, for you thought it would be equivalent to an admission of your having been guilty of the charge of disrespect imputed to you by Sir John Franklin ; and also on the ensuing day, when I showed you the draft of the letter entreating further inquiry, and of which you also disapproved, you said that *Lady Franklin was trifling* with you, that you had given her an opportunity of retracing her steps, and that if she did not avail herself of it *she must take the consequences.* I concluded with you in the opinion that there was no longer much hope of a reconciliation, but suggested that you were not then in a position, without actual proof of insincerity, to say anything against her. You differed from me, but what you said I have forgotten; even the previous particulars had not come to my recollection when I wrote my statement, and therefore it is that I mention them now.

I am not at all prepared to contend with you as to the claim which you prefer to the possession of a more retentive memory. Were mine very retentive, the events and conversation of the period in question would, I am ready to admit, notwithstanding the excitement and agitation which prevailed, and in the very vortex of which I was placed, have left more numerous and distinct impressions upon my mind.

But I should do myself a positive injustice did I omit to make the observation, that, to say the least, I was quite unprepared for the assumption of superior accuracy on your part, and indeed surprised at it.

To your concluding paragraph and allusion to Sir Eardley Wilmot, the meaning of which it is impossible to mistake, and which I exceedingly regret, the most obvious answer appears to be the simple remark, that the fears you have expressed have proved to be groundless, and that had you been aware of all the circumstances connected with my treatment after I left the office of Treasurer, you could not possibly have entertained them.

I have carefully perused your Memorandum ; my recollection differs from yours on several points, but the two following are the only instances in which I appear to have any personal interest, and to which it is therefore incumbent upon me to advert :—

I *distinctly* recollect that you did not allude to any previous conversation when you requested me to wait upon Lady Franklin, and I have no recollection of the conversation you have mentioned, neither do I believe that any such ever did take place.

I *never* stated that Lady Franklin would effect the reconciliation upon two conditions, and I *never* proposed to you the conditions which you have recorded. I would have cut off my right hand sooner.

But I see from the result that I myself have greatly erred in one particular. I acted for the best, but I ought to have sent you my statement; by not doing so I have perhaps inflicted both on you and myself a serious wrong. You might have seen from it how much your own recollection must be at fault. I had been previously reminded, too, more than once by Mr. Forster, of the necessity of furnishing you with it; in order to correct any error, so far as it is yet possible, I now send it to you. It is, I assure you, not without extreme concern that I feel it to be impossible under existing circumstances to address you otherwise than as

Your very obedient Servant,

ADAM TURNBULL.

REPLY TO PETITION FOR DR. COVERDALE'S RESTORATION.

To the Rev. W. J. Aislabie (Chaplain of the Richmond District).

Colonial Secretary's Office, October 22, 1841.

SIR,—1 am directed by the Lieut.-Governor to acknowledge the receipt of the communication of the 14th instant, signed by yourself and twenty-five inhabitants of the district of Richmond, in which you state, that without questioning the propriety of His Excellency's decision, arising out of the lamentable death of Richard Higgins, you will be thankful if His Excellency will restore Dr. Coverdale to the appointment which he lately held.

I am to inform you, that having considered the request of so many of the most respectable inhabitants of your district, including the Foreman of the Jury on the Inquest, the Lieut.-Governor has, in compliance with your desire, thus unanimously and respectfully communicated to him, thought proper to comply with your request by returning Dr. Coverdale to his former office.

I have, &c. &c.,

JOHN MONTAGU.

Mr. Aislabie's Reply.

Richmond, October 25, 1841.

SIR,—I have the honour to acknowledge the receipt of your letter of the 22nd instant, in which you inform me that "the Lieut.-Governor has, in compliance with your desire, thus unanimously and respectfully communicated to him, thought proper to comply with your request by returning Dr. Coverdale to his former office."

In the name of those inhabitants who signed the letter of the 14th instant, and of those now made acquainted with its purport who had no opportunity of signing it, I return His Excellency the warmest thanks for his compliance with their request, and I shall take care that every one of them shall see your letter, that all may know the handsome terms in which this favour has been conveyed.

For myself I can unfeignedly say, that no public act by which I have been affected has ever given me so great satisfaction.

I have the honour, &c. &c.,

W. J. AISLABIE.

To the Colonial Secretary.

Rev. Mr. Aislabie to Mr. Montagu.

Richmond, February 7, 1842.

MY DEAR SIR,—I think it due to Sir John Franklin and to yourself that an error in the 'Courier' of the 4th instant should be immediately corrected by me *.

---

* *Extract from a "Précis" published in the Hobarton 'Courier' Newspaper, Friday, Feb. 4, 1842.*

*   *   *   In the beginning of October Sir John and Lady Franklin went to the Richmond district, where her ladyship remained several days, and during that period a private petition was got up to Sir John Franklin to restore Dr. Coverdale, and about the end of October he was restored accordingly, without any reason whatever being assigned for such an act of grace.

Captain Montagu, it is understood, submitted to the Lieut.-Governor

That paper contains, "that in the beginning of October Sir John and Lady Franklin went to the Richmond district, where her ladyship remained several days, and during this period a private petition was got up to restore Dr. Coverdale."

It is untrue that a petition was got up during Lady Franklin's stay in the district, and equally untrue that Lady Franklin had anything to do with it, or that I, with whom the letter originated, took my idea from any other person. I will relate all I know about it.

We heard that Sir John Franklin would stay in Richmond three hours on his way to Mr. Parsons': when, however, I proceeded to the inn, intending to pay my respects to him, and, if possible, to speak to him concerning Dr. Coverdale's case, I found that he had passed on. I afterwards saw Lady Franklin once, who honoured us with a morning visit; Dr. Coverdale's name was not mentioned.

I had not framed any further intention on the matter, until one evening something led me to ask, or Dr. Coverdale to offer, a perusal of the papers referring to it. Having perused them, without making known my intention to any person, I proceeded to Hobarton the following morning, when His Excellency granted me an interview*, and at its conclusion told me he would see the principal medical officer. I believe this was on the 13th of October, for on the 14th of that month I wrote and procured signatures to the letter requesting the reinstatement of Dr. Coverdale.

Hence you see how greatly the writer in the 'Courier' must have been misinformed as to the date and origin of the letter, and how false his position, that "the correspondence which ensued upon the subject of necessity caused the name of Lady Franklin to be introduced."

I feel certain that justice to all parties demands this earliest possible refutation of the statement in the 'Courier' of the 4th instant. I

---

that the course pursued upon the occasion was very undesirable, as tending to lower the dignity and character of the Government.

The correspondence which ensued upon the subject of necessity caused the name of Lady Franklin to be introduced, in consequence of which, offence being taken, an apology was demanded by her ladyship† from the Colonial Secretary, and by him, under all the circumstances of the case, absolutely declined.

* Lady Franklin knew nothing of Mr. Aislabie's application to me, nor did I say anything to her on this subject, till the Richmond Memorial, which I decided on complying with, was before me.

---

† No apology was demanded.

shall therefore send a copy of it for the information of His Excellency the Lieut.-Governor.

I remain, dear Sir,
Yours very truly,
W. J. AISLABIE.

Mr. Montagu to Sir John Franklin.

Newlands, February 8, 1842.

SIR,—The Rev. Mr. Aislabie having acquainted me that he has transmitted to Your Excellency a copy of a letter dated yesterday, which he has addressed to me, I feel it to be right to furnish Your Excellency with a copy of my reply to that gentleman, and which I have now the honour to enclose.

I have the honour, &c. &c.,
JOHN MONTAGU.

His Excellency, Sir John Franklin.

Copy of Letter Enclosed.

Newlands, 8th February, 1842.

MY DEAR SIR,—I beg to acknowledge your letter of yesterday.

For the statements in the 'Courier' or in any other newspaper, I am not responsible, and should not have noticed that to which you allude; but I feel I am bound to notice a statement from yourself, and to inform you that I, as well as others, have read in Lady Franklin's handwriting that she did suggest to Mrs. Parsons the private petition in Dr. Coverdale's case, and you are aware that a private petition* was subsequently adopted, and succeeded.

In making this announcement, I beg you will understand that I have no intention of impugning your statement of your own conduct, and you will perceive that yours is not inconsistent with Lady Franklin's account of her own upon the subject of the petition.

As you have forwarded a copy of your letter to Sir John Franklin, I shall follow your example, and send His Excellency a copy of this note.

I remain, dear Sir,
Yours truly,
JOHN MONTAGU.

To Rev. W. J. Aislabie.

---

* There was but one petition or letter, or communication presented in Dr. Coverdale's case, i. e. the one written and presented by the Rev. Mr. Aislabie.

APPENDIX.

A.

AFTER some preliminary observations in favour of Mr. Montagu, 'Civis' writes: "On taking that position on the receipt of the memorandum, he (Mr. M.) must have been aware of the utter irreconcileableness of it with the altered views of the Lieutenant-Governor towards the object aimed at by the censure passed on Mr. Macdowell; and if so, he must have been further aware that, consistently with his feelings as a gentleman, his honour as a man, or his dignity as the representative of Her Majesty, the Lieutenant-Governor was bound, after such an avowal of his sentiments, to see that the next officer in his government did cordially and effectually second and support him in those his altered views. And even it may be regretted that some calm looker-on was not invited to the discussion whose experience and knowledge of the world would have softened asperity and induced a better understanding of the grounds of the irritation, under the effects of which His Excellency most justifiably dictated the memorandum in question. Had this been done, I cannot for a moment believe but that Captain Montagu himself would have admitted the change in His Excellency's sentiments towards Mr. Macdowell was forced upon him by an imperative necessity which knew no control; at least, all would admit that the constant weekly vituperation, supported by a masterly flow of ironical ratiocination which acknowledged no authority of reason or common sense, was such that His Excellency would have undoubtedly derogated from his honour to have longer borne it without evincing the strongest, nay, the sternest marks of his displeasure.

"To whom could he address those marks of his displeasure for instant development and operation but the Colonial Secretary? By what unaccountable process of reasoning could that officer have brought his mind to the conclusion that any gentleman, after such an expression of dissatisfaction, would, by any means whatever, be induced to retract his words, to make his denouncement, and to submit to the eternal disgrace of witnessing his government, purse and family exposed to a sharpness and bitterness of animadversion most galling to his feelings? The conclusion is inevitable. The Lieutenant-Governor having taken his determination, and the Colonial Secretary his position, it must have been evident to those acquainted with the circumstances, that from that moment either Sir John Franklin must resign or the Colonial Secretary be removed. . . . . . . Then why assume an attitude of self-defence, the sole effect of which would only be to screen Mr. Macdowell from the effects of His Excellency's displeasure?

" I am not the censor of the press ; such an office is not within the category of a Colonial Secretary's duties. My best ability is puzzled by the *bizarre* situation in which so inconceivably strange a memorandum places me. In short, I do not understand your memorandum ; and to be plain at once, I will take no step whatever in furthering the denunciation you have been pleased to thunder at the devoted head of Mr. Macdowell. Such was instantly, no doubt, under a perfect consciousness of his own innocence, evidently the view Captain Montagu took of His Excellency's memorandum, and any third-class boy of common capacity must have foreseen that the only result must be (and be so understood by both) that one of the combatants, either the Lieutenant-Governor or himself, must retire from the field.

" CIVIS."

B.

In Mr. Macdowell's letter to Lord John Russell, of July 31st, 1841, soliciting the reconsideration of his lordship's judgement, he writes : " Your lordship will feel, I am persuaded, that no complaint of that kind (disrespect) was ever in His Excellency's thoughts, so far as I was concerned. His Excellency, I feel alike convinced, read my letter in the consciousness of what was due from me, not less to his high station and characteristic urbanity than to his unfailing kindness to me personally. . . . . . I have ever found Sir John Franklin an indulgent master ; I have served him according to my poor abilities faithfully ; it would ill become me, if I possessed the power, in this colony, to forget his kindness when I was no longer permitted to partake of it."

C.

" February 9th, 1843.

" MY DEAR —, I have since you left seen copies of the despatch No. 150, to Sir John, as also of Lord Stanley's letter to Capt. Montagu, enclosing it and Capt. Montagu's reply, the latter being one of the most extraordinary productions I ever saw, giving Sir John a few final stabs, more severe than any preceding ones could be.

" I have no doubt whatever that this is a verbatim copy of the despatch, and not mere extracts; indeed Lord Stanley's letter to Capt. Montagu states that he encloses a copy of the despatch he has sent to Sir John Franklin, *and it must have been the style and tenor of that document which could have induced Capt. Montagu to address so extraordinary a letter to Lord Stanley in reply.* These various documents are now circulated throughout the colony and shown to all, as also *a statement of a personal interview between Capt. Montagu and the Secretary of State, wherein of course the Governor does not stand in the most favourable light."*

D.

Mr. Thomas Young to Mr. Henslowe.

10 Liverpool Street, July 13, 1843.

SIR,—I have to acknowledge receipt of your letter of yesterday's date, enclosing me copies of two letters addressed by Mr. Thomson to Mr. Price, on the subject of Captain Montagu's correspondence with Lord Stanley, intimating that you were commanded by the Lieut.-Governor to transmit me the same, and to request that I would favour His Excellency with any observations that might suggest themselves to me.

I was determined for various reasons to make no written communication in this matter. Since I formed that resolution, however, a very material change of circumstances has taken place. I have been placed by 'Murray's Review' before the public, as one of seven who have read the book, and week after week, I find myself along with the others referred to, to testify to the most unblushing falsehoods,—that the correspondence bound up in the Book does not contain the statements quoted in the 'Advertiser' newspaper. I am thus directly made a party to this statement if I do not speak out *.

* The following extract from a Number of 'Murray's Review' illustrates Mr. Young's observation:—
" It has been industriously reported that the Book contains some letters and statements detrimental to Lady Franklin. The report is entirely unfounded: that lady's name is never mentioned but incidentally and necessarily in the course of Capt. Montagu's defence, and then only in relation to those matters which were fully given to the public in this journal at the time. Now this is a faithful *précis* of the whole contents of this ' *book,*' about which, we repeat, so much and so ridiculous an outcry has been raised. We ask any man of ordinary understanding, be his party what it may, under what pretence Capt. Swanston could have forwarded to Lord Stanley a collection of documents, the original of every one of which is already at the Colonial Office,—copies of the very book itself in the hands of Capt. Montagu's numerous friends in England, —copies of it *we know* received by the mess of the Royal Artillery, both United Service Clubs, and many other quarters; *we know* also that a copy of ' the despatch ' is in the possession of Sir George Gipps at Sydney, and we have reason to believe a copy of the very book itself. We assure the Government House clique that they will find no difficulty in obtaining the book in England; and therefore we again ask, upon what possible pretence could Capt. Swanston have forwarded to Lord Stanley a 'verified' copy of a book, every word contained in which has been already brought under his consideration, the original document deposited in his lordship's office, and the book itself, we have no doubt, in his lordship's hands, it being in the hands of every individual connected with these colonies in England? We assure the semi official that we have above afforded him a full and accurate *précis* of the contents of the book."— *Murray's Review*, June 16, 1843.

L

Another reason induces me to answer your communication, and that is, before the correspondence formed the subject of newspaper controversy, I spoke of its contents to many individuals. Justice to myself therefore on both grounds compels me to answer your communication. His Excellency is well aware that he is entitled to no courtesy at my hands.

I received the correspondence from Captain Swanston along with a note requesting me to return it to him after I had perused it. The note only expresses "correspondence," not "and notes of conversation," as erroneously stated by Mr. Thomson in this particular. This note I showed to Mr. Thomson in vindication of myself against the insinuations of the 'Review.' The correspondence was not solicited by me, but I understood was thus sent to me by Mr. Swanston in reference to a conversation I had with him on the subject of the result of it, in the decision of Lord Stanley, as that bore upon the position of Dr. Turnbull, in the relation which he stood to His Excellency, having thereby apparently turned his back on his old friend. Captain Swanston also held a similar conversation with the Rev. Mr. Lillie and Dr. Officer, the latter gentleman having first spoken to me on the subject. The very nature of this conversation was to induce me to speak to Dr. Turnbull. I did so, and in doing this, it became necessary for me to disclose to him a certain portion of the correspondence.

I also mentioned to him that Lady Franklin was spoken of in disparaging terms, without representing to him the exact expressions.

After having perused the correspondence I sealed it up, and returned it to Captain Swanston without having shown it to any one, or having made any extract from it. I had read aloud, however, certain very pungent parts of it to Mrs. Young and my daughter, and unless Captain Swanston believed me to be indeed a perfect anchorite, how could he suppose that I could resist gratifying the female portion of my household by withholding from them such very exciting portions of the book? He never dreamt that I was to seal it up in my own bosom;—of what value was it there? Accordingly I considered myself at perfect liberty to speak of it freely, and I did so to many individuals, and indeed the subject formed the general topic of conversation. That I was entitled to do so, Captain Swanston very frankly admitted to me, as well as to Dr. Turnbull, to whom he stated that the book was not sent to me to be perused in secret, and that I was at liberty to make the communication to him which I did: this was in answer to a question put to Captain Swanston by Dr. Turnbull in reference to this communication. It is very plain, therefore, that if I have stated that the book contains any of the statements alleged by the 'Advertiser' to be contained in it, but which are now positively denied by 'Murray's Review,' that I receive the "lie direct" if I hold my peace. This is a powerful motive to open one's mouth. Not that I am the least anxious to give Mr. Murray a public denial, for it is well known here that his statements of facts are generally purely imaginative. I am anxious, however, so far as I am concerned, that those individuals to whom I have spoken of the correspondence may know that I now reiterate the statements which I formerly made, some of which I find correctly stated in the ' Advertiser,' but which are now so unblushingly denied by the ' Review.' And I am the more induced to do this, as the continued reite- ration by Mr. Murray of the denial of these statements seems to imply that he is sanctioned by the Custodier of the Book to make them. This I cannot however believe, but I am disappointed in not having seen a public denial from Captain Swanston on this subject.

I have therefore to state that Mr. Thomson has (substantially) cor- rectly asserted the statements which I made to him, with one or two slight mistakes. The verbal statements referred to are said to be " con- versations " with Lord Stanley. There are, however, no rejoinders from Lord Stanley, so far as I can recollect; the whole are merely statements said to have been made to Lord Stanley by Captain Montagu : you will perceive the distinction in this.

When I read the phrase " intriguing, mischievous, bad woman," in the ' Advertiser,' I exclaimed in the presence of Mrs. Young and my daughter, " That is too bad : Captain Montagu does not state that in the book :" they both exclaimed at the same time, " Well, you read us that from the book." Upon repeating this to the Rev. Mr. Lillie, he at once stated, " I noted these expressions, as well as the others asserted in the ' Advertiser ' as to pandering." Mr. Lillie has since explained to me, that he is not so clear as to the words *intriguing* and *mischievous*, but that he clearly and distinctly recollects the epithet of " bad woman " being applied to Lady Franklin, in that part of the book which records the verbal statements.

The statements contained in Mr. Thomson's second letter are also substantially correct. In the same record of the verbal statements, Sir John Franklin is represented as a " mere imbecile," and " that it is only necessary to see him to be convinced of the fact." This evidence of course His Excellency will carry along with him, and Lord Stanley will be able to appreciate its accuracy.

After having perused the Book, I stated to Capt. Swanston that I considered it highly honourable in Capt. Montagu having recorded in it the verbal statements which he made to Lord Stanley, in order that his friends and others might see the *whole case upon which his lord- ship had arrived at his decision.*

I regret exceedingly that Capt. Swanston has not deemed it proper to forward His Excellency a copy of the Book. This was the true way to have tested its accuracy, and to have made Capt. Montagu stand upon high ground. I almost now feel ashamed at having been one of the privileged few, in being favoured with the perusal of a successful defence which is not allowed to face its opponent.

The low, taunting, boasting bravado of the 'Review' on this head is quite in keeping with its editor's other statements on the subject; but I cannot allow myself to believe that Capt. Swanston has authorized him to make such a proposition of giving a copy provided it be published in the 'Gazette.' If a sincere desire to give it so great a publicity exists, why complain of a lesser publicity having been given to it? The publication in the 'Gazette,' however, is so utterly absurd, as to prove the total want of sincerity in the offer.

I cannot conclude without stating, that I experienced a feeling of loathing in reference to one part of His Excellency's treatment of Capt. Montagu. In His Excellency's communication to Capt. Montagu, suspending him from his office, he states, that although he was forced to adopt the measure in consequence of Capt. Montagu's entanglement through his local prejudices and interests in this place, yet he was happy to bear testimony in his favour as to his usefulness, and that he would represent to the Secretary of State that he had no doubt he would efficiently fill a similar honourable office elsewhere, where these prejudices and interests referred to did not interfere. I quote the instance you will perceive from memory. Now at the very time that this letter was written, it appeared to me that the St. George's Tower Despatch was got up, from its having immediately followed Capt. Montagu's departure, and in which despatch he is accused of having imposed upon and deceived His Excellency in having contracted for the erection of the Tower upon a second plan, by which the Government would have been put to an enormous additional expense, contrasted with the first plan, of which His Excellency only knew and approved of. The hypocrisy of the first statement, as contrasted with the last, appeared to me truly disgusting. I must say, however, that after the recent discovery of the mediation through Dr. Turnbull, that Capt. Montagu has excelled His Excellency in this respect. The beseeching prayer of Capt. Montagu to obtain Lady Franklin's mediation to restore him to office, and to the confidence of His Excellency, and which appears to have been so readily and generously granted by her ladyship, makes a sad contrast with his subsequent slander of that lady's character: the utter baseness of the man, in having so acted under the circumstances, is beyond all comment.

I enclose you the copy of Mr. Thomson's letters, having referred to them in connection with this letter, and I have to request that you will forward a copy of this letter and of Mr. Thomson's to Capt. Swanston.

I have the honour, &c. &c.,

THOMAS YOUNG.

F. H. Henslowe, Esq.,
Private Secretary.

Mr. Henslowe to Mr. Young.

Government House, July 14, 1843.

Sir,—I have the honour, by desire of the Lieut.-Governor, to acknowledge the receipt of your letter of yesterday's date, together with the copies of Mr. Thomson's letters which you have returned, and which, with your communication, will be forwarded according to your request to Capt. Swanston.

His Excellency observes in your communication one passage involving a misrepresentation of so serious a nature, that it cannot be allowed to remain on record unaccompanied by a fitting refutation.

You are pleased to say, that " at the very time when Sir John Franklin's letter to Mr. Montagu was written," conveying to that gentleman the expressions of kindness produced on the part of His Excellency by too confiding a generosity, "the St. George's Tower Despatch was *got up.*"

The *facts* of the case are as follows:—On the 17th December 1841, Capt. Cheyne sent in a somewhat elaborate remonstrance against his suspension, in which the question of St. George's Church formed a prominent part.

His Excellency, without going into this document, sent it to Mr. Montagu for his observations, who returned it on the 30th of December.

His Excellency was prevented by press of business from giving this subject any further consideration for some days; when he did however inquire into it, so much mystery and confusion appeared, as to render it quite unintelligible.

On the 19*th of January*, His Excellency requested that the Colonial Secretary would procure for him the various *plans*, and the authority upon which Capt. Cheyne had commenced the erection of the *large Tower*, and additional alterations then in progress, for His Excellency knew that he had never given any such authority, but as yet had no cause to suspect any one of misconduct except Capt. Cheyne.

Mr. Montagu's reply on the 24th January was, that he *had been unable to succeed in finding the plans*, and that *he had never seen* the authority upon which the erection of the large Tower had been commenced.

Before the arrival of the last mentioned memorandum Mr. Montagu had been suspended, and on the 1st of February, in answer to Mr. Montagu's earnest representations, His Excellency was induced to address him in the terms to which you refer.

About the same time as the above-named reply, Mr. Montagu forwarded to His Excellency a letter from the Rev. Mr. Fry, dated 23rd January, in which *it was stated* that *he* (Mr. Fry) had *submitted the plans* to His Excellency and *received his approval of them.*

This it was in His Excellency's power by collateral evidence to disprove, but Mr. Montagu nevertheless rested upon Mr. Fry's evidence, to show that the Lieut.-Governor had *himself* approved the plans.

On the *tenth of February* Mr. Montagu sailed.

On the *eighth*, for the first time, Capt. Cheyne, who had been charged by the Lieut.-Governor with commencing the alterations without authority, stated in reply that he had received both verbal and written instructions from the Colonial Secretary.

On the 14th of February, four days after Mr. Montagu's departure, His Excellency, still as much as ever in the dark, sent a series of questions to the Colonial Secretary to be propounded and answered. Nor was it until the 19th that His Excellency received information of such a nature, as to lead him to put an immediate stop to the works. He was still seeking for information, and for the *plans, which could not be found*, but which were at length discovered some days after,—on what precise day does not appear,—and *for the first time submitted to His Excellency*.

It was then that Sir John Franklin forwarded to the Secretary of State, on the 6th of March, the despatch which he had commenced on the 26th of February, and which was written with no view of influencing Mr. Montagu's case, but, as in duty bound, to elucidate Captain Cheyne's; and upon every principle of justice, His Excellency was bound, when at length in possession of the facts, to exonerate Captain Cheyne from the blame which had been attached to him.

Two points remained to be cleared up. In *June* 1842, four months after Mr. Montagu's departure, Mr. Fry wrote to His Excellency to express his " regret at having made an erroneous statement " in reference to the *plan* which he supposed he had submitted to His Excellency, and to explain that the plan could not have been submitted by him, as he first stated to Mr. Montagu.

In *May last* (1843), fifteen months after Mr. Montagu's departure, Captain Cheyne produced a letter from Mr. Montagu in which that gentleman had urged him to send the plans *for the Lieutenant-Governor's approval.* The plans were sent, but Mr. Montagu stated in January 1842, *that he had never seen any authority.* These papers have been submitted to the Right Honourable the Secretary of State.

Upon the terms in which your inferences upon this subject are couched, His Excellency deems no comment to be necessary.

I have, &c. &c.

F. H. HENSLOWE,
Private Secretary.

Thomas Young, Esq.,
Liverpool Street.

Mr. Young to Mr. Henslowe.

10 Liverpool Street, 18th July, 1843.

Sir,—I have the honour to acknowledge the receipt of your letter of the 14th instant, conveying to me by command of His Excellency an explanation of the circumstances connected with the St. George's Tower Despatch. After having expressed myself in the strong terms I did to you in my letter of the 13th instant in reference to this subject, I feel it due to His Excellency, after he has favoured me with this explanation, to state to His Excellency through you my opinion regarding it. And in doing this, it gives me much pleasure to say that my sentiments on the subject are entirely changed.

The explanation which you have given is most ample and satisfactory, and this has been much strengthened since by a communication being made to me by Captain Cheyne, of the discovery of the original order to him by Captain Montagu to proceed with the erection of the second tower. I now perceive that His Excellency has been grossly maligned by Captain Montagu in his defence to Lord Stanley on this subject.

And on another point I am equally satisfied that His Excellency has been as greatly traduced. The success of such a defence as this has proved itself to be, upon two points which bear materially upon the character and complexion of all the rest, it is to be hoped will only be short-lived.

After such a conviction being produced on my mind, I feel it due to my own self-respect, as well as in justice to His Excellency, to make this candid acknowledgement, and to request that the expressions of disrespect which I used in my letter to you of the 13th instant, in so far as they referred to His Excellency, may be considered as withdrawn.

I have the honour, &c. &c.,

Thomas Young.

F. H. Henslowe, Esq.,
Private Secretary.

E.

INSCRIPTION

FOR THE FOUNDATION-STONE OF CHRIST'S COLLEGE,

VAN DIEMEN'S LAND, NOVEMBER 7, 1840.

Christo Dicatam
Hanc Omnis Humanitatis et Scientiæ Domum
Johannes Franklin Eq. PH., Eq. R., LL.D. R.S.S.
Insulæ Tasmaniensis Præses
Consilii Sententia Impensis Coloniæ Fieri Jussit
Lapidem Auspicalem Posuit
Anno Victoriæ Quarto
vii Id. Nov. MDCCCXL.

Interfuere Viri Spectatissimi Ex Utroque Consilio
Gulielmus Henricus Elliott Eq. H. Milit. Præfect.
Johannes Lewes Pedder Eq. Aur. Justiciarius Principalis
Gulielmus Hutchins M.A. Archidiaconus
Matthias Forster Secretarius
Adam Turnbull Thesaurarius
Josias Spode Irenarches
Edvardus Macdowell Procurator Regius
Georgius Thomas Gulielmus Blaney Boyes Rationalis
Georgius Henricus Barnes Portitoriis Conquirendis Præpositus
Thomas Anstey
Thomas Archer
Carolus Swanston
Carolus Maclachlan
Gulielmus Effingham Lawrence
Gulielmus Page Ashburner
Michael Fenton
Juventuti Educandæ Præposito Johanne Philippo Gell M.A.
Operum Publicorum Curatore Alexandro Cheyne

Jacobus Clark Ross Et Huic Comes Franciscus Crozier
Per Ignota Septentrionalis Oceani
Anglorum Perenne Nomen Laturi Incepto Bene Auspicato
Lubenter Interfuere

G.

July 1, 1841.

MY DEAR SIR,—Agreeably to your desire, the plans of the new portico, spire, and other improvements for St. George's Church, have been submitted to Mr. Fry, Mr. Hone and Mr. Barnard, who have authorized me to say, that they, with myself, highly approve of the design, and respectfully request your assistance in effecting its completion.

Yours, &c.,

CHARLES D. LOGAN.

J. Montagu, Esq.,
Colonial Secretary.

Endorsed on the above note is the following order in Mr. Montagu's handwriting :—

CAPT. CHEYNE is now authorized to proceed with the work as speedily as possible, and if anything should occur to delay its progress, he will have the goodness to report the cause to me for the Lieutenant-Governor's information.

JOHN MONTAGU,
July 2, 1841.

H.

Extracts from Mr. Montagu's Letter of 16th of January 1844.

No. 1.

I sent to Van Diemen's Land two copies of Lord Stanley's despatch to Sir John Franklin which contained his lordship's decision upon my case. When I received your letter of 17th of September 1842, transmitting to me a copy of that despatch, I felt I had a right to show it to whom I pleased. I imagined it was sent to me for that purpose, to enable me to satisfy those who were aware of my suspension from office, that I had obtained a complete and honourable acquittal. I did not hesitate to distribute many copies for that purpose in England. I did it openly, and sent them to several persons with whom I knew Lord Stanley associated, and through whom I doubted not his lordship would, and perhaps did, hear of the use I had made of his despatch. For the same reason I sent two copies to Van Diemen's Land, one to Mr. Forster and one to Captain Swanston. I requested them to show it to my friends, and to those who took an interest in my case * ; but I stipulated that no newspaper was to have one word of the despatch communicated to it †.

I begged that it might not be used in triumph over Sir John Franklin. Having obtained justice, I was satisfied, and desired not to do anything which might wear the appearance of conveying to him reproach or humiliation ‡. My only motive was to satisfy the minds of my friends, and those who under trying circumstances had continued their confidence in me.

No. 2.

With respect to the bound folio book which had been shown to various persons by one of my friends, I admit that I sent it to Van Diemen's Land for the following reasons :—Lord Stanley no doubt remarked, in reading the documents in my case, which passed between Sir John Franklin and myself before my departure from Van Diemen's Land, that he suspended me from office without furnishing me with a specific definite charge. I left the colony without in fact knowing the actual fault imputed to me §. Under this state of things, a few of my

---

* A direction to which Captain Swanston probably understood he might give a liberal interpretation, since the despatch lay at the Derwent Bank for general inspection.

† See note at p. 48. The ' Courier' newspaper, which first published Lord Stanley's despatch, must have derived it either from Mr. Forster or Captain Swanston, or must have had a third copy of its own.

‡ An observation which shows Mr. Montagu's perfect apprehension and calculation of the nature and tendency of the despatch.

§ This excuse is a plausible one to those who are ignorant of facts. But Lord Stanley, who has the voluminous correspondence before him which passed between Mr. Montagu and me before Mr. Montagu left Van Diemen's Land, and also all the counteracting statements, testimonies and vouchers with which Mr. Montagu provided himself, cannot make, and has not made this amongst the other excuses his lordship has adduced for Mr. Montagu's conduct. Nay, more : Lord Stanley, by adducing the St. George's Church case as one of which Mr. Montagu had no notice before he left Van Diemen's Land, virtually contrasts it with the other charges of which he was cognizant, and thus contradicts Mr. Montagu's assertion. (See No. 150.) Nevertheless I may remark, that the subtle character of Mr. Montagu's conduct was such as to make it extremely difficult to embody as specific charges, that thorough disaffection, and those minute but incessant reticences of duty which were productive of more serious impediments in the admi-

most intimate friends being anxious to know the full particulars of the charge against me, and what might transpire upon it in England, I promised I would send them a copy of my correspondence with the Colonial Office. The book referred to by Sir John Franklin contains that correspondence, and with the exception of the two memoranda in it to which I will presently refer, I pledge you my honour it does not contain one single word beyond copies of the letters I wrote to the Colonial Department and of those I received from it on this subject*. The book I sent to Van Diemen's Land by Mr. Bicheno, and requested him to deliver it to Mr. Forster. In my letter transmitting it, I told Mr. Forster that I sent it for the perusal of a few particular friends, for their personal information, in accordance with my promise, and that I wished it to be considered quite private. He repeated my injunctions upon delivering it to Captain Swanston, who treated it as requested†. He writes to Lord Stanley,—" The documents were forwarded to me for my own personal information. The papers Mr. Montagu has sent me were entirely confidential communications. I have shown the book to none but a very few of Mr. Montagu's personal friends, and gentlemen only to whose character and reputation Sir John Franklin himself bears ample testimony ‡." To the best of my recollection, I requested Mr. Forster to show the correspondence to Captain Swanston, a most sincere friend, to whom I am under many obligations ; to Sir John Pedder, a dear and sincere friend of nearly twenty years' standing ; and to Mr. Charles Arthur, Mrs. Montagu's cousin, the police magistrate of Norfolk Plains. In thus using this correspondence, I did not feel that I was in the slightest degree acting contrary to custom in such cases. I did not intend to violate any official usage. I considered it as my private property, and that I was at liberty to use it at my discretion. I can solemnly declare, that in sending it out I had no wish, no intention

---

nistration of affairs than a more open opposition would have been. I have explained to Lord Stanley that this is by no means inconsistent with the acknowledgement of the services which Mr. Montagu rendered when under the obligation of his oath in the Executive Council ; but this Mr. Montagu has endeavoured to bring forward against me.

* Mr. Montagu does not state how large a portion of a folio book containing 312 pages was occupied by his memoranda ; nor does he seem to feel that when these were left out of consideration, there was no occasion to pledge his honour to the contents of what remained.

† See pp. 55 and 56.

‡ Mr. Swanston has not stated whether he includes under the term of Mr. Montagu's " personal friends " and under the terms which follow, Mr. Robert Lathrop Murray, and one or two others whose names I refrain from mentioning.

of annoying or prejudicing Sir John Franklin or his government in any way whatsoever*.

No. 3.

The first time I had the honour of seeing Lord Stanley was on the 29th of August 1842. He then informed me that he should not confirm Sir John Franklin's act of suspension. As I did not expect a more formal announcement of the issue of my case, and being naturally anxious to communicate it to my friends and relations, I drew up a memorandum, which does not contain, as Sir John Franklin has represented, Memoranda and Minutes of Conversations between Lord Stanley and me, but merely the substance of the decision in my case, as communicated to me by Mr. Hope and Lord Stanley, with certain statements I made to them, without adding any observations of theirs thereupon.

This memorandum I circulated in England amongst some of the persons to whom I have already stated I sent a copy of the despatch. As soon as I received your letter of the 17th September 1842, transmitting Lord Stanley's despatch, which you informed me I was to consider as conveying to me his lordship's decision upon my case, I stopped circulating the Memorandum, and putting it with the Correspondence, thought no more about it.

Unfortunately, I did not separate it, as I ought to have done, from the correspondence, and a copy of it was sent with the other documents to Van Diemen's Land. I can assure you most positively, that when I put it with the letters, I had no intention of sending it to Van Diemen's Land. On the contrary, I had determined not to make any farther use of it, after the receipt of the Despatch, but it was copied with the other documents, and passed unobserved†. I would here remark, that the fact of the book containing this memorandum having been sent by me for the perusal of a few intimate friends, will easily account for a species of inattention to it, which could not be claimed for it, if a more public or a more extended one had been contemplated; but having no such object in view, and my mind being exceedingly occupied with pressing business at the time, I did not give proper consideration to it, which I now extremely regret.

---

* See contents of Mr. Young's letter, and other illustrations of the temerity of Mr. Montagu's assertion.

† See Appendix (C.), where it appears, by a private letter from a gentleman residing in the colony to his friend, of a date several months *antecedent* to the arrival of the memorandum in the book, that a statement, similar to that memorandum, was then current in the colony.

No. 4.

It is not my intention to justify having sent that memorandum to Van Diemen's Land. I cannot defend it. I was wrong, and I am sorry for having been so thoughtless*.

---

* It seems superfluous to make any comments on this embarrassed statement: at one time, one of Mr. Montagu's memoranda slips into his book, and gets bound up in it unobserved; at another time, it would appear to have been a wilful error which he cannot defend. Nothing is attempted to be said of the introduction of the other memorandum. The whole leaves, I think, but one impression on the mind,—that of a consciousness on Mr. Montagu's part of great delinquency, from which he did by no means foresee that Lord Stanley would so easily relieve him.

THE END.

Printed by Richard and John E. Taylor, Red Lion Court, Fleet Street.

www.ingramcontent.com/pod-product-compliance
Ingram Content Group UK Ltd.
Pitfield, Milton Keynes, MK11 3LW, UK
UKHW042152280225
455719UK00001B/295